# THE PENNSYLVANIA
# BOXING HALL
# OF FAME

Four of the best light heavyweight boxers of the 1970s and 1980s gathered at the 2011 Pennsylvania Boxing Hall of Fame (PABHOF) induction ceremony in Philadelphia. From left to right are Mike Rossman, former World Boxing Association champion; Matthew Saad Muhammad, former World Boxing Council champion; Jerry Martin, three-time world title challenger; and Richie Kates, two-time world title challenger. Both Martin and Kates were inducted at this event. Saad Muhammad (PABHOF 2005) and Rossman (PABHOF year uncertain) were previous inductees. (Photograph by John DiSanto.)

FRONT COVER: Harry Greb was Pennsylvania's greatest boxer. (Author's collection.)

COVER BACKGROUND: The Met was an important Pennsylvania boxing venue in the 1940s and 1950s. (Peltz Boxing Promotions.)

BACK COVER: Pictured are Pennsylvania Boxing Hall of Famers Joey Giardello (left) and George Benton. (Author's collection.)

# THE PENNSYLVANIA BOXING HALL OF FAME

*John DiSanto*

ARCADIA
PUBLISHING

*For great friends recently lost, especially Stanley "Kitten" Hayward,*
*Carmen "Bartsy" Bartolomeo, and Michael "Airplane" Connor.*

Copyright © 2024 by John DiSanto
ISBN 978-1-4671-6082-7

Published by Arcadia Publishing
Charleston, South Carolina

Printed in the United States of America

Library of Congress Control Number: 2023943064

For all general information, please contact Arcadia Publishing:
Telephone 843-853-2070
Fax 843-853-0044
E-mail sales@arcadiapublishing.com

Visit us on the Internet at www.arcadiapublishing.com

# CONTENTS

# ACKNOWLEDGMENTS

I want to acknowledge the Veteran Boxers Association–Ring One (VBA) for the opportunity to be a part of the Pennsylvania Boxing Hall of Fame. I joined the PABHOF committee in 2006 and was appointed its chairman in 2013. Three different VBA administrations trusted me to lead the PABHOF, and that experience gave me the unique perspective I brought to this book.

Thank you to the photographers whose work is the highlight of this publication. They include Darryl Cobb Jr., Jano Cohen, Ray Bailey, Jim Rogge, and Pete Goldfield. There are also numerous unknown photographers whose images fill my filing cabinets—and this book. They remain unidentified in these pages, but I appreciate their work and cherish the photographs they left behind. Others who contributed images include Peltz Boxing Promotions, Richard Pagano, Jimmy Deoria, the Front Street Gym, Carol Polis, George Silvano, Vincent Ciaramella, Johnny Gilmore, and Chuck Hasson. I also want to thank Henry Hascup, Matthew H. Ward, and J Russell Peltz, who fact-checked the details, corrected many errors, and offered general feedback that helped me shape this book. Thank you to my editor Caroline (Anderson) Vickerson and everyone at Arcadia Publishing. Finally, thank you to my wife, Jennifer DiSanto, who encouraged me to push forward with this project when my focus, energy, and motivation occasionally wavered.

Throughout the book, I use many abbreviations including KO (knockout), KOs (knockouts), TKO (technical knockout), PABHOF (Pennsylvania Boxing Hall of Fame), IBHOF (International Boxing Hall of Fame), BWAA (Boxing Writers Association of America), USBA (United States Boxing Association), NABF (North American Boxing Federation), AAU (Amateur Athletic Union), PAL (Police Athletic League), WBC (World Boxing Council), WBA (World Boxing Association), IBF (International Boxing Federation), WBO (World Boxing Organization), and NBA (National Boxing Association). In boxing, the meaning of the phrase "world champion" has evolved over the years. For simplicity's sake, in this book, I refer to any fighter who won at least a portion of a world title as a world champion.

# INTRODUCTION

The Pennsylvania Boxing Hall of Fame was established in 1958 by members of the Veteran Boxers Association–Ring One to honor the elite members of the state's boxing community. VBA president Joe Guinan headed the first Pennsylvania Boxing Hall of Fame committee, which selected a five-member inaugural class of inductees: Billy Conn, Harry Greb, Tommy Loughran, Philadelphia Jack O'Brien, and Lew Tendler. On April 3, 1958, an event to announce the new class was held at Lew Tendler's restaurant in Philadelphia.

The PABHOF committee continued to select new members annually and celebrated the occasion with an induction ceremony and banquet. In the early years, with decades of boxing history already in the books and a vast field of potential inductees available, the choices made were all sound. Prominent figures including Leo Houck, Harry Lewis, Frank Klaus, Herman Taylor, Johnny Jadick, Benny Bass, and Fritzie Zivic entered the PABHOF in the years immediately following.

The banquet proved to be a major source of fundraising for the VBA, and its attendance grew larger and larger each year. For many years, the site of the banquet was Palumbo's, a popular South Philadelphia restaurant, nightclub, and expansive banquet facility. The PABHOF event became an exciting night out for the honorees, VBA members, boxing fans, and the community.

However, the commercial potential of the event and the fact that it was the biggest single revenue source for the VBA began to impact who was chosen for induction. To help keep the event a moneymaker, new inductees were often picked for their ticket-selling potential or their association with the VBA. This began to hurt the credibility of the PABHOF.

Although many justified inductees were honored, a list of glaring omissions quickly grew. Many worthy boxers were overlooked while judges, politicians, lawyers, businessmen, and minor fighters made the cut. Also, the relative lack of African American inductees suggested that racism might be affecting the selection process. As decades passed, the list of hall of fame members became cluttered with lesser-known people who had been inducted for dubious reasons.

As this silent policy continued and further diluted the essence of the PABHOF, a spin-off group headed by Willie and Becky O'Neill, a married couple who trained and managed boxers, formed the Pennsylvania State Boxing Hall of Fame in the 1970s. For several years, they inducted their own set of honorees at a separate annual event. Some of their selections included Tyrone Everett, Tommy Cross, Willie Reddish, Johnny Hutchinson, and J Russell Peltz. Eventually, this second organization and its hall of fame folded while the PABHOF continued.

In 2005, I joined the VBA. Although I never boxed, I was accepted as a member because of my work as a boxing writer and historian. One year later, John Gallagher, then VBA vice president and chairman of the PABHOF, asked me to join the PABHOF committee. I eagerly accepted but expressed my concerns about the selection methods and the many omissions the PABHOF had made. I stressed that if I joined the effort, I planned to act as an advocate for those who were excluded, both living and dead, and would try to improve the PABHOF process. Knowing that changes were due, Gallagher agreed.

The first step was to reconstruct a complete list of all Pennsylvania Boxing Hall of Fame inductees, which had not been kept up to date. With help from historian Chuck Hasson, we compiled the full list using vintage PABHOF programs and newspaper archives. Next, at the 2006 ceremony, the PABHOF officially absorbed, or re-inducted, those individuals who had been elected by the spin-off group.

Working closely with Gallagher, I eventually steered the PABHOF to a more objective process. We implemented a ballot system, which shifted the decision-making process from a small group of VBA insiders to an organized voting body. This new voting body included historians, writers, previous inductees, knowledgeable boxing people, and VBA members. The result was positive, with the quality of inductee classes drastically improving.

In 2013, I succeeded Gallagher as PABHOF chairman. At that time, I instituted the use of various metrics to help measure the quality of nominees. Specific requirements were installed to help eliminate individuals with thinner resumes who might be considered because of their involvement with the VBA or other irrelevant factors.

A conscious effort was also made to nominate forgotten boxers as well as trainers, promoters, managers, writers, cutmen, and other non-boxers, all of whom were previously ignored. Later, we created a nomination committee to expand our perspective, better evaluate candidates, and solidify the overall process.

The new controls created much conflict between the VBA membership and the PABHOF committee. Some pressured for a return to the old ways. Others requested a loosening of the new rules to allow wider eligibility for nominees not meeting the revised standards. Believing that the new measurements were fair, the committee held firm and kept the new process in place. However, a set of logical exceptions was introduced to allow further discussion for borderline candidates. These amendments did not guarantee any individual would reach the ballot but did offer an opportunity for further advocacy if desired.

Although still an imperfect system, our efforts over the past 18 years have resulted in a more rational, stable, ethical, and fair election process. Previously ignored champions (including Larry Holmes, Jeff Chandler, Charlie Brown, Gary Hinton, and Robert Hines), contenders (including Bennie Briscoe, Mike Everett, and Dick Turner), and critical non-boxers (including Joe Gramby, Quenzell McCall, Jimmy Wilson, and Eddie Aliano), as well as many others from every previous era and category were elected under the new process.

Further, the number of non-White inductees significantly increased under the new system, which began taking root in 2006. From 1958 to 2005, a total of 228 people were inducted, 21 of them non-White (nine percent). Between 2006 and 2023, a total of 210 individuals were inducted, including 129 non-Whites (61 percent). The new system was also in effect when the first three female inductees (Jacqui Frazier-Lyde, Lynne Carter, and Carol Polis) were welcomed into the PABHOF.

Although the new system helps to protect the selection process from the old behaviors that once impeded it, friction still exists. Since the annual banquet is still the largest fundraising event for the VBA, some continue to argue that a candidate's revenue-generating potential should outweigh pure merit. I believe this dynamic would only cease if the PABHOF became independent from the VBA. Although I have advocated for this measure, this course has not yet been taken.

In 2023, the PABHOF, the longest-running boxing hall of fame in the country, celebrated its 65th induction class. The new 16-member class brought the total number of inductees to 438.

The goal of this book is to document everyone honored by the PABHOF. However, the format of the publication only allows space for photographs and descriptions of about half of all the inductees. Therefore, omissions exist in each of the five chapters. To help remedy this, a complete list of PABHOF members is included. The result is the most comprehensive Pennsylvania Boxing Hall of Fame reference to date. I hope you enjoy this book and find it informative, interesting, and entertaining.

# 1

# WORLD CHAMPIONS AND INTERNATIONAL HALL OF FAMERS

Born in Ukraine, Benny Bass (PABHOF 1964, IBHOF 2002) immigrated to Philadelphia as a boy and became a professional boxer by age 15. The "Little Fish" participated in more than 200 professional bouts from 1919 to 1940 and eventually won both the featherweight and junior lightweight world titles. Barely over five feet tall, Bass was a hard-punching action fighter who fought the best of his era. He died in 1975 at age 71. (Author's collection.)

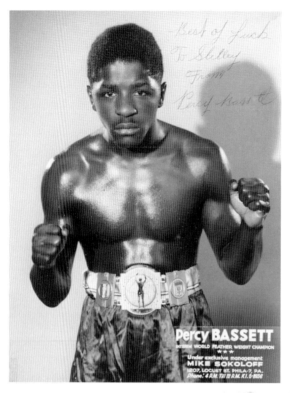

Born in Virginia, Percy Bassett (PABHOF 2008) grew up in Philadelphia and became a number one–ranked featherweight boxer during the 1950s. He won the "Interim" world featherweight championship in 1953 while champion Sandy Saddler served in the US Army. He held the title until 1954 but never received a chance to fight Saddler. A detached retina forced the end of Bassett's career (1947–1955). He was 25 years old with a record of 64-12-1 (41 KOs). He died in 1993 at age 63. (Author's collection.)

Known as the "Mayor of North Philadelphia" and the "Professor," George Benton (PABHOF 1986, IBHOF 2001) was one of Pennsylvania's best, and most avoided, middleweights (1949–1970). Once rated third in the world, Benton defeated three future world champions: Joey Giardello, Jimmy Ellis, and Freddie Little. However, he never received a title shot. After retiring with a record of 61-13-1 (36 KOs), Benton became a trainer, guiding nearly 20 fighters to world championships. He died in 2011 at age 78. (Author's collection.)

Born in Kentucky, Jack Blackburn (PABHOF 1977, IBHOF 1992) fought more than 300 professional bouts (1900–1923), including fights against legends Harry Greb, Joe Gans, Sam Langford, Philadelphia Jack O'Brien, Kid Norfolk, and Harry Lewis. Despite this distinguished career in the ring, Blackburn is best remembered as the trainer of heavyweight champion Joe Louis. Blackburn also trained world champions Sammy Mandell and Bud Taylor. Blackburn died in 1942 at age 59. (Author's collection.)

Charles "The Hatchet" Brewer (PABHOF 2008) won the vacant IBF super middleweight championship in 1997 with a TKO of Gary Ballard. He successfully defended his title three times, including the only world title fight ever held at the Blue Horizon, a famous Philadelphia venue. After losing the title to Sven Ottke, Brewer, born in 1969, earned three more title opportunities. He retired in 2005 with a record of 40-11 (28 KOs). (Author's collection.)

Charlie "Choo Choo" Brown (PABHOF 2010) began his career (1979–1993) with 23 wins in his first 26 bouts. He won the first-ever IBF lightweight championship in 1984 with a 15-round decision over Melvin Paul. Brown, born in 1958, was 22 years old. He lost the belt in his first defense to Harry Arroyo. The defeat initiated his decline, with Brown winning only three of his final 17 fights. He retired with a record of 26-16-2 (18 KOs). (Photograph by Pete Goldfield.)

Pittsburgh-based welterweight Charley Burley (PABHOF 2013, IBHOF 1992) scored major wins over Fritzie Zivic, Billy Soose, Holman Williams, Leon Zorrita, Young Gene Buffalo, and Archie Moore. Despite these impressive victories, he never received a title shot during his career (1936–1950). Instead, Burley claimed the "Colored Welterweight Title" with a 15-round victory over Cocoa Kid in 1938. His overall record was 83-12-2, 50 KOs, and one no contest. He died in 1992 at age 75. (Author's collection.)

Jeff Chandler (PABHOF 2006, IBHOF 2000) won the WBA world bantamweight championship in 1980 with a TKO of Julian Solis. "Joltin' Jeff," born in 1956, successfully defended the title nine times, including wins over Solis, Gaby Canizales, Johnny Carter, Jorge Lujan, Eijiro Murata, Miguel Iriarte, and Oscar Muniz. He lost the belt to Richie Sandoval in 1984 and immediately ended his career (1976–1984) with a record of 33-2-2 (18 KOs). (Author's collection.)

Born George Chipulonis in New Castle, Pennsylvania's George Chip (PABHOF 2016) fought more than 160 times as a professional (1909–1921). In 1913, he knocked out Frank Klaus to claim the world middleweight championship and later defeated Joe Borrell and Klaus in a rematch. Chip held the crown until 1914 when he was defeated by Al McCoy in Brooklyn, New York. Chip died in 1960 at age 72. (Author's collection.)

Writer Nigel Collins (PABHOF 2012, IBHOF 2015) was born in England in 1946 but worked primarily in the Philadelphia area throughout his accomplished career. He began covering boxing for numerous publications during the 1970s. In 1983, Collins became the assistant editor of *The Ring* and was promoted to editor in chief two years later. After four years, Collins left *The Ring*, only to return in 1993. He served as editor in chief for another 18 years. Collins also authored the books *Boxing Babylon* (1990) and *Hooking Off the Jab* (2022). (Photograph by John DiSanto.)

"The Pittsburgh Kid," Billy Conn (PABHOF 1958, IBHOF 1990), posted an overall record of 63-11-1 (15 KOs) during his career (1934–1948). He won the light heavyweight championship in 1939 with a decision over Melio Bettina and defended this title three times. He relinquished the crown in 1941 when he challenged heavyweight champion Joe Louis. Conn was ahead on points when Louis knocked him out in round 13. Conn lost the rematch in 1946 after serving in World War II. He was elected to the inaugural classes of both the PABHOF and the IBHOF. He died in 1993 at age 75. (Author's collection.)

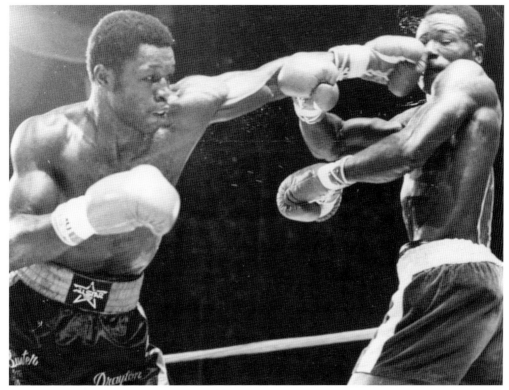

Hard-hitting junior middleweight Buster "The Demon" Drayton (PABHOF 2003, left) won the IBF world title by 15-round decision over Carlos Santos in 1986. He defended twice, including a TKO of Davey Moore, before losing the belt by decision to Matthew Hilton in 1987. Drayton scored other victories over Clint Jackson, Mark Kaylor, and John Jarvis (right). He also faced Terry Norris, Julian Jackson, and James Kinchen during his career (1978–1995). Drayton's final record was 40-15-1 (28 KOs). He died in 2022 at age 70. (Author's collection.)

Brothers Chris Dundee (PABHOF 1978, IBHOF 1994, real name Mirena, left) and Angelo Dundee (PABHOF 1977, IBHOF 1992) were South Philadelphia natives who had a huge impact on boxing. Angelo, one of the sport's great trainers, guided 16 world champions, including Muhammad Ali, "Sugar" Ray Leonard, Carmen Basilio, Jose Napoles, Luis Rodriguez, and Willie Pastrano. Active from 1955 to 2005, Angelo died in 2012 at age 90. Chris Dundee was a manager and promoter who worked with Ken Overlin, Dick Welsh, Midget Wolgast, and others. In 1950, he opened his famous Fifth Street Gym in Miami Beach. He died in 1998 at age 91. (Author's collection.)

Beginning in the 1950s, Don Elbaum (PABHOF 2011, IBHOF 2019) promoted or copromoted more than 1,000 fight cards, from club shows to championships, all over the world. He either promoted, matched, or advised numerous boxers, including "Sugar" Ray Robinson, Willie Pep, Aaron Pryor, Tony Tubbs, Simon Brown, Maurice Blocker, and David Telesco. Born in 1931, Elbaum was the house matchmaker during the final chapter of the Blue Horizon and is also credited with getting Don King into the boxing business. (Photograph by John DiSanto.)

New Orleans native Bernard Fernandez (PABHOF 2005, IBHOF 2020) began covering boxing for the *Philadelphia Daily News* in 1984. He became a boxing writer and columnist in 1987 and held the position for 25 years. Fernandez, born in 1947, covered local action as well as major fights worldwide. He served as the president of the Boxing Writers Association of America for four terms and has won several awards. He also published *Championship Rounds*, a five-volume anthology of his work. (Photograph by Darryl Cobb Jr.)

Joe Frazier (PABHOF 1991, IBHOF 1990) was an Olympic gold medalist as an amateur and world heavyweight champion as a professional (1965–1981). He defeated Buster Mathis, Jimmy Ellis, Jerry Quarry, George Chuvalo, Bob Foster, and, in the "Fight of the Century," Muhammad Ali in 1971. Frazier and Ali battled twice more in their epic trilogy (1971–1975). In one of the best-ever heavyweight eras, Frazier posted an overall record of 32-4-1 (27 KOs). He died in 2011 at age 67. (Author's collection.)

"Sister Smoke" Jacqui Frazier-Lyde (PABHOF 2014), the daughter of "Smokin' " Joe Frazier, was the first woman elected to the PABHOF. As a professional boxer, she earned world title belts at super middleweight (2002), light heavyweight (2001), and heavyweight (2004). She even faced Laila Ali (Muhammad Ali's daughter) in a high-profile showdown marketed as Ali-Frazier IV. Born in 1961, Frazier fought between 2000 and 2004 and posted an overall record of 13-1 (9 KOs). (Photograph by Pete Goldfield.)

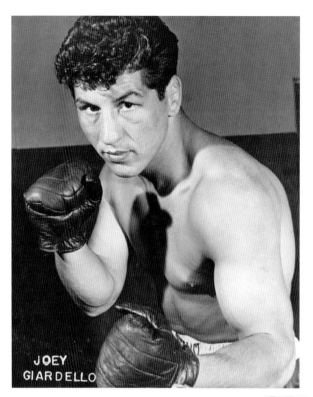

JOEY
GIARDELLO

Born Carmine Tilelli in Brooklyn, Joey Giardello (PABHOF 1972, IBHOF 1993) was a perennial middleweight contender who finally won the world championship in 1963 after more than 120 professional bouts. After taking the title from Dick Tiger in 1963, Giardello defended it against Rubin "Hurricane" Carter before losing it back to Tiger in 1965. After four more fights, Giardello retired (1948–1967) with a record of 98-26-8, one no contest, and 31 KOs. Giardello died in 2008 at age 78. (Author's collection.)

Born Feab Williams in Mobile, Alabama, George Godfrey (PABHOF 2011, IBHOF 2007) was a popular heavyweight contender based in Leiperville, Pennsylvania, whose potential was limited because he was African American. Although he won most of his 120 bouts between 1919 and 1937, Godfrey was never granted a title fight. He faced Sam Langford, Primo Carnera, Jack Sharkey, and Paolino Uzcudun and was a worldwide attraction both as a boxer and a wrestler. Godfrey died at age 50 in 1947. (Author's collection.)

The relentless "Pittsburgh Windmill," Harry Greb (PABHOF 1958, IBHOF 1990), fought 299 bouts and is considered one of the greatest fighters in boxing history. He won the middleweight championship in 1923 and made six defenses. Blind in the right eye and with vision fading in the left, Greb lost his title to Tiger Flowers in 1926. He retired after losing their rematch. Greb died from complications following eye surgery in 1926 at age 32. He defeated 12 world champions, including Gene Tunney, Tommy Loughran, Mickey Walker, Maxie Rosenbloom, and Battling Levinsky during his career (1913–1926). (Author's collection.)

Southpaw Robert "Bam Bam" Hines (PABHOF 2009) posted a record of 25-3-1, 17 KOs, and one no contest during his nine-year career (1981–1990). On his way up the ranks, Hines, born in 1961, won the USBA junior middleweight title in 1987. In 1988, Hines became a world champion with a 12-round decision over Matthew Hilton. He lost the championship in his first defense to Darrin Van Horn in 1989. The brittle hands that plagued Hines throughout his career were a factor in his early retirement. (Photograph by Pete Goldfield.)

"The Easton Assassin," Larry Holmes (PABHOF and IBHOF 2008, right), won the first 48 bouts of his professional career (1973–2002). In 1978, Holmes took the WBC heavyweight championship from Ken Norton and remained champion for seven years, making 20 title defenses. His challengers included Muhammad Ali, Earnie Shavers, Gerry Cooney, Mike Weaver, Tim Witherspoon, and David Bey (left). After losing the title to Michael Spinks in 1985, Holmes, born in 1949, earned five more world title opportunities, and closed his career with a record of 69-6 (44 KOs). (Author's collection.)

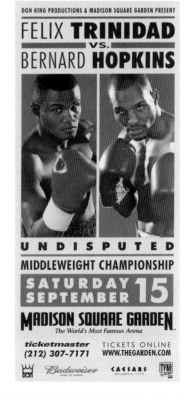

Bernard Hopkins (PABHOF 2022, IBHOF 2020) held a world middleweight championship for 10 years and set a division record with 20 title defenses. Hopkins, born in 1965, moved up in weight and won the light heavyweight championship and fought until he was nearly 52 years old. He was the oldest boxer to ever win a world title and the oldest ever to unify or defend a world title. His record of 55-8-2, 32 KOs, and two no contests is loaded with great opponents. (Author's collection.)

Born John Jadich in Ukraine, Johnny Jadick (PABHOF 1963) began fighting professionally at 15 and had 164 professional bouts (1923–1937). In 1932, Jadick won the world junior welterweight title with a decision over Tony Canzoneri at home in Philadelphia. However, after nine months, the NBA decided to no longer recognize junior weight divisions. This left Jadick an ex-champion without having lost his title. He also faced Louis "Kid" Kaplan, Benny Bass, and Lew Massey. Jadick died in 1970 at 61. (Author's collection.)

Harold Johnson (PABHOF 1974, IBHOF 1993) beat Jimmy Bivins, Tommy Ruth, Arturo Godoy, and Archie Moore early in his professional career (1946–1971). Johnson won the NBA light heavyweight title in 1961 with a knockout of Jesse Bowdry. He received universal recognition as world champion in 1962 after defeating Doug Jones. Johnson was also a ranked contender as a heavyweight but never received a title shot in that weight class. He retired with a 76-11 record (31 KOs). He died in 2015 at age 87. (Author's collection.)

Born Barney Lebrowitz in 1891, Battling Levinsky (PABHOF 1967, IBHOF 2000) was a skillful boxer who had nearly 300 bouts during his career (1910–1930). He won the light heavyweight championship in 1916 with a 12-round decision over Jack Dillon and held the title for four years. Levinsky also faced Leo Houck, Billy Miske, Gunboat Smith, Harry Greb, Jack Dempsey, Gene Tunney, and Young Stribling. He also fought under the name Barney Williams. Levinsky died in 1949 at age 57. (Author's collection.)

Harry Lewis (PABHOF 1959, IBHOF 2008) was born Henry Besterman in New York. He began boxing professionally at age 17 and fought more than 160 times (1903–1913). Lewis claimed the world welterweight championship in 1908. He defended the crown six times before relinquishing the title in 1911. He faced Joe Gans, Young Erne, Jack Blackburn, Unk Russell, Frank Klaus, Leo Houck, and Georges Carpentier. In his final bout against Joe Borrell, Lewis was severely injured and retired immediately afterward. Lewis died in 1956 at age 69. (Author's collection.)

Tommy Loughran (PABHOF 1958, IBHOF 1991) held the light heavyweight championship from 1927 to 1929 before relinquishing the title to pursue the heavyweight crown. He defeated former heavyweight champions Max Baer and Jack Sharkey but failed in his challenge of reigning champion Primo Carnera in 1934. Considered one of the greatest fighters in boxing history, Loughran faced 13 world champions and had more than 170 bouts during his career (1919–1937). He died in 1982 at age 79. (Author's collection.)

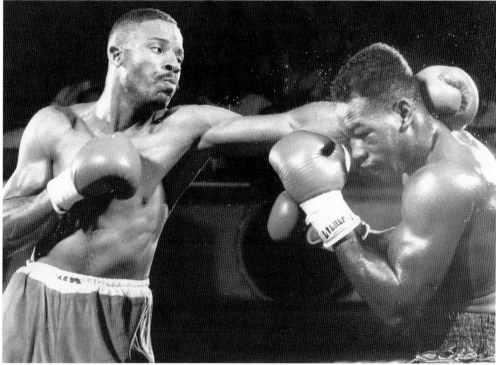

Nate "Mr." Miller (PABHOF 2002, left) won the NABF cruiserweight regional title in 1989 with a TKO of Bert Cooper. Six years later, Miller, born in 1963, won the WBA world title with an eighth-round knockout of Orlin Norris in London. After four successful defenses, Miller lost his crown to Fabrice Tiozzo by decision in 1997. His career (1986–2001) record was 31-9 (27 KOs). Miller is pictured with Andre McCall. (Author's collection.)

THE PENNSYLVANIA BOXING HALL OF FAME

"Bobcat" Bob Montgomery (PABHOF year uncertain, IBHOF 1995) won the world lightweight championship twice during his career (1938–1950). In 1944, Montgomery defeated Beau Jack to take the world title. Jack (left) regained the belt later that year. Montgomery won the title a second time with a 1944 victory over Jack and held the title until 1947. Montgomery won the Pennsylvania state title in 1939 and had memorable rivalries against Jack (2-2), Ike Williams (1-1), Lew Jenkins (1-1), and Wesley Mouzon (1-1). He retired with a record of 75-19-3 (37 KOs). He died in 1998 at age 79. (Author's collection.)

Born James Hagen in Philadelphia in 1878, Philadelphia Jack O'Brien (PABHOF 1958, IBHOF 1994) fought nearly 200 bouts during his career (1896–1912), capturing the light heavyweight championship in 1905. O'Brien fought in every division between lightweight and heavyweight and faced many great boxers, including Jack Johnson, Bob Fitzsimmons, Stanley Ketchell, "Barbados" Joe Walcott, Sam Langford, Joe Choynski, Peter Maher, Marvin Hart, Joe Butler, Tommy Burns, and Jack Blackburn. O'Brien died in 1942 at age 64. (Author's collection.)

Promoter J Russell Peltz (PABHOF 2006, IBHOF 2004) began his career at age 22 at the Blue Horizon in 1969. In 1973, Peltz, born in 1946, became the director of boxing for the Spectrum and staged more than 70 shows there through 1980. Peltz played a part in the Atlantic City boxing boom of the 1980s, promoting many events at various casino venues. In his 50-year promotional career, Peltz developed several champions, including Jeff Chandler, Matthew Saad Muhammad, Mike Rossman, Charles Brewer, Marvin Johnson, Kasim Ouma, and Jason Sosa. He chronicled his career in his 2021 memoir *Thirty Dollars and a Cut Eye*. (Photograph by Pete Goldfield.)

Philadelphia native "Fearless" Freddie Pendleton (PABHOF 2022) was a late bloomer who fought 53 professional bouts over the first 12 years of his career (1981–2001) before finally winning the IBF world lightweight championship in 1993. He successfully defended the title once before losing it in 1994. Born in 1963, Pendleton also won the Pennsylvania and USBA regional lightweight titles and the USBA regional junior welterweight title, and earned five other world title fights. He retired with a record of 47-26-5 (35 KOs). (Photograph by Pete Goldfield.)

Born Dwight Braxton in Baltimore, Dwight Muhammad Qawi (PABHOF 2010, IBHOF 2004) won the WBC world light heavyweight championship with a 1981 knockout of Matthew Saad Muhammad. He made three successful defenses before losing to WBA champion Michael Spinks in a 1983 title unification fight. Qawi, born in 1953, moved up to the cruiserweight division and won the WBA world cruiserweight title in 1985. Later, Qawi won the WBC Continental Americas regional cruiserweight title twice. He retired with a 41-11-1 (25 KOs) record. (Photograph by Pete Goldfield.)

"The American Dream," David Reid (PABHOF 2011), won a gold medal at the 1996 Olympics. Before turning professional, Reid, born in 1973, required surgery to repair an eyelid injury. Fearing more eye complications, Reid rushed his career (1997–2001) from the start. After just 10 bouts, Reid won a regional title belt, which propelled him into a WBA world title fight against Laurent Boudouani. Reid won the title by decision and made two defenses. In 2000, he lost the title to Felix Trinidad. Reid had surgery to repair a detached retina and only fought four more times. He retired with a record of 17-2 (7 KOs). (Author's collection.)

"The Jewish Bomber," Mike Rossman (PABHOF year uncertain), became WBA light heavyweight champion with a TKO of longtime champion Victor Galindez in 1978. He made one successful defense against Aldo Traversaro in 1978 before Galindez regained the title in a 1979 rematch. Born in 1956, Rossman had a memorable 10-year career (1973–1983), with fights against Mike Quarry, Lonnie Bennett, Mike Nixon, Yaqui Lopez, Tony Licata, and Dwight Muhammad Qawi. He finished with a record of 44-7-3 (27 KOs). (Author's collection.)

One of the most exciting fighters of all time, Matthew Saad Muhammad (PABHOF 2005, IBHOF 1995, left) had an uncanny ability to recover from heavy punishment. He fought back from the brink of defeat numerous times on his way to winning the WBC light heavyweight title against Marvin Johnson in 1979. As champion, he continued to wage memorable wars against Yaqui Lopez, John Conteh, Jerry Matin, and Dwight Muhammad Qawi. His career (1974–1992) resulted in a 39-16-3 (29 KOs) record. He is pictured with Richie Kates and referee Charles Sgrillo (PABHOF 1986). Muhammad died in 2014 at age 59. (Author's collection.)

Steve "Double S" Smoger (PABHOF 2013, IBHOF 2015) was one of the busiest and most highly regarded referees in the sport. His career as a referee (1984–2018) included more than 1,000 bouts and more than 200 world title contests. He reportedly worked in more American states and foreign countries than any other professional referee in history. Smoger worked bouts with ring greats Larry Holmes, Roberto Duran, Mike Tyson, Roy Jones Jr., Bernard Hopkins, James Toney, and Felix Trinidad. Smoger died at age 79 in 2022. (Photograph by Pete Goldfield.)

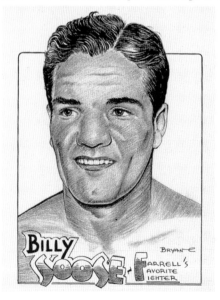

Born in Farrell, Pennsylvania, Billy Soose (PABHOF 1963, IBHOF 2009) was an outstanding amateur before turning professional (1938–1942). He beat world champions Ken Overlin and Tony Zale in two 1940 nontitle bouts, which earned him the reputation as the "uncrowned champion." In a 1941 rematch, Soose won the New York state version of the world middleweight championship in an upset of champion Ken Overlin. Five bouts later, Soose walked away from the sport and joined the US Navy. He died in 1998 at age 83. (Author's collection.)

Known as "The Pittsburgh Kid," Paul Spadafora (PABHOF 2020) was a tough southpaw who did not lose a fight until the next to last bout of his career (1995–2014). Born in 1975, Spadafora won the IBF lightweight championship in 1999 and defended the title eight times. He gave up the belt to move up in weight. Late in his career, Spadafora also won the NABF junior welterweight regional title and retired with an overall record of 49-1-1 (19 KOs). (Author's collection.)

Herman Taylor (PABHOF 1961, IBHOF 1998) promoted boxing shows at every major Philadelphia venue between 1912 and 1975, including bouts featuring Lew Tendler, Tommy Loughran, Benny Leonard, Mickey Walker, Benny Bass, and "Sugar" Ray Robinson. In 1952, Taylor staged three massive outdoor events over a four-month period at Municipal Stadium: Jersey Joe Walcott defended his heavyweight championship against Ezzard Charles (June), Kid Gavilan defended his welterweight crown against Gil Turner (July), and Rocky Marciano won the heavyweight title from Walcott (September). Taylor died in 1980 at age 93. (Author's collection.)

Meldrick Taylor (PABHOF 2008) won an Olympic gold medal in 1984 at age 17. He quickly climbed the professional ranks (1984–2002) and won the IBF junior welterweight championship against Buddy McGirt in 1988. In his fifth defense, Taylor, born in 1966, suffered a heartbreaking TKO loss against Julio Cesar Chavez with two seconds remaining in the final round. Taylor went on to win the WBA welterweight championship in 1991 and defended it twice. He fought long past his prime and finally retired with a record of 38-8-1 (20 KOs). (Author's collection.)

Lightweight southpaw Lew Tendler (PABHOF 1958, IBHOF 1999) is considered one of the greatest boxers never to win a world championship. He defeated numerous contenders during his career (1913–1928) but lost two decisions against champion and all-time great Benny Leonard in 1922 and 1923. He later challenged another legend, Mickey Walker, for the welterweight title but again lost by decision. He fought more than 170 bouts and was inducted by the PABHOF in its inaugural class. Tendler died in 1970 at age 72. (Author's collection.)

"Terrible" Tim Witherspoon (PABHOF 2008) was a two-time world heavyweight champion during his career (1980–2003). After just 15 fights, Witherspoon, born in 1957, challenged WBC heavyweight champion Larry Holmes and almost won the title in the close 1983 bout. Witherspoon won the vacant WBC heavyweight title against Greg Page in 1984. Although he lost the belt in his first defense, Witherspoon won his second world title in 1986 against Tony Tubbs. Witherspoon defended against Frank Bruno before losing the title to James Smith in 1986. He retired with a record of 55-13-1 (38 KOs). (Author's collection.)

Born Joseph LoScalzo, Midget Wolgast (PABHOF 1968, IBHOF 2001) won his first share of the flyweight championship in 1930 at age 19. He added the New York version of the title two months later. Wolgast drew with NBA champion Frankie Genaro in a unification bout but defended against Willie LaMorte and Ruby Bradley during his reign as champion. He outgrew the flyweight division in 1934 and made an unsuccessful attempt at the bantamweight crown in 1935. He fought another five years, retiring (as a welterweight) after more than 200 bouts between 1925 and 1940. Wolgast died in 1955 at age 45. (Author's collection.)

Teddy Yarosz (PABHOF 1972, IBHOF 2006) of Monaca, Pennsylvania, won the world middleweight championship in 1934. Yarosz took the Pennsylvania version of the crown by 15-round decision over Jimmy Smith before adding the New York state version and the NBA world middleweight title with a 15-round decision over Vince Dundee. Yarosz also scored wins over Archie Moore, Billy Conn, Paul Pirrone, and Ken Overlin during his career (1929–1942). His final record was 107-18-3 (17 KOs). Yarosz died in 1974 at age 63. (Author's collection.)

"The Croat Comet," Fritzie Zivic (PABHOF 1966, IBHOF 1993, left), won the world welterweight championship in 1940, defeating Henry Armstrong over 15 rounds. He stopped Armstrong in a rematch before losing the title on points to Freddie Cochrane in 1941. During his 233-bout career (1931–1949), Zivic faced many top fighters, including "Sugar" Ray Robinson, Jake LaMotta, Johnny Jadick, Lou Ambers, Eddie Cool, Billy Conn, Charley Burley, Sammy Angott, Bummy Davis, Lew Jenkins, Beau Jack, Bob Montgomery, and Billy Arnold (right). Zivic died in 1984 at 71. (Author's collection.)

# 2

# WORLD TITLE
# CHALLENGERS

London-born southpaw Bobby Barrett (PABHOF 1966) grew up in Philadelphia and fought 94 professional bouts as a welterweight between 1920 and 1931. He posted early wins against Eddie Dempsey, "Oakland" Jimmy Duffy, Joe Welling, and Joe Tiplitz. After beating Ray Mitchell (twice) and Nate Goldman and drawing with Lew Tendler, Barrett faced Mickey Walker for the NBA world welterweight championship in 1924. Walker defended his title by sixth-round knockout. Barrett died in 1972 at age 71. (Author's collection.)

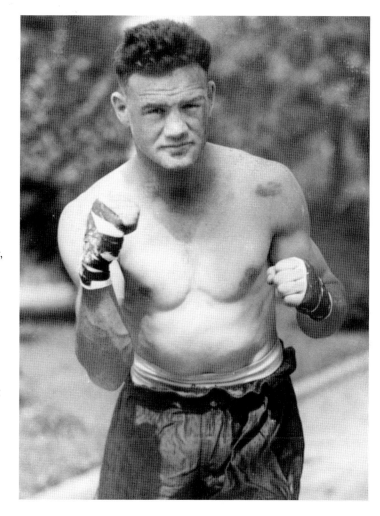

Philadelphia heavyweight David "Hand Grenade" Bey captured the USBA regional title with a victory over Greg Page, earning him a crack at IBF world champion Larry Holmes in 1985. Bey (PABHOF 2017) started quickly and proved tough early in the bout. However, the undefeated champion scored two knockdowns and stopped Bey in round 10. It was the Philadelphian's first loss. He retired in 1994 with a record of 18-11-1 (14 KOs). Bey died in a work-related construction accident in 2017 at age 60. (Photograph by Pete Goldfield.)

Tyrell Biggs (PABHOF 2013) won an Olympic gold medal in 1984 and went on to win his first 15 professional fights, including wins over James Tillis, Jeff Sims, Renaldo Snipes, and David Bey. In 1987, Biggs, born in 1960, fought Mike Tyson in Atlantic City for the world heavyweight championship. He lost the fight by TKO in round seven. In subsequent bouts, Biggs unsuccessfully tried for the USBA regional title twice against Mike Hunter and Buster Mathis Jr. He retired in 1998 with a record of 30-10 (20 KOs). (Author's collection.)

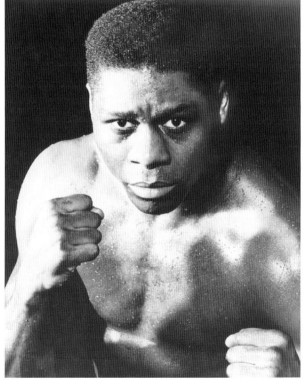

Italian-born Johnny Bizzarro (PABHOF 2016) came from a multigenerational fighting family from Erie, Pennsylvania. The most accomplished boxer of the family, Bizzarro won the North American junior lightweight title and twice challenged for a world title. In 1963, he lost a 15-round decision to champion Flash Elorde in Manilla. His second shot came against Carlos Ortiz in 1966. Ortiz defended the title by a 12th-round TKO. Bizzarro retired in 1968 with a final record of 55-11-2 (24 KOs). He died at age 60 in 1998. (Author's collection.)

The younger brother of Johnny Bizzarro, Lou Bizzarro (PABHOF 2022) earned a world title bout after opening his career with 22 straight victories. His big opportunity came at home at Erie's County Field House against Roberto Duran. The great WBA lightweight world champion Duran defended his title by knockout. Bizzarro lasted until the 14th round when he was knocked out by the all-time great. Bizzarro, born in 1946, won nine of his final 10 bouts and retired in 1982 with a 31-2 (9 KOs) record. (Photograph by Darryl Cobb Jr.)

One of the toughest fighters never to win a world title, "Bad" Bennie Briscoe (PABHOF 2007) earned three chances at the middleweight crown during his 20-year career (1962–1982). He lost decisions to champions Carlos Monzon (1972) and Rodrigo Valdez (1977) and was knocked out by Valdez in 1974. Briscoe was Pennsylvania state champion at welterweight and middleweight and won the North American middleweight title. His final record was 66-24-5 with one no contest and 53 KOs. Briscoe died in 2010 at age 67. (Author's collection.)

Johnny "Dancing Machine" Carter (PABHOF 2012) was one of the best American bantamweights of the 1980s. Unfortunately, his career (1978–1989) coincided with the career of *the* best bantamweight of the era, fellow Philadelphian Jeff Chandler. Carter, born in 1957, challenged Chandler in a 1982 title fight but lost by TKO in round six. Carter won the Nevada and USBA bantamweight regional titles, both in 1980. He also won the Pennsylvania junior featherweight belt in 1985. He retired in 1989 with a 33-8 (21 KOs) record. (Photograph by Pete Goldfield.)

Randall "Tex" Cobb (PABHOF 1997) was a popular heavyweight contender who competed as a professional kickboxer before becoming a traditional fighter. He won his first 17 bouts, including a TKO of Earnie Shavers, before losing two in a row to Ken Norton and Michael Dokes. However, after three more wins, Cobb, born in 1953, landed a bout with Larry Holmes for the WBC world heavyweight championship in 1982. The tough-chinned Cobb lost a 15-round decision. He fought for another 11 years and finished with a record of 42-7-1 (35 KOs). (Author's collection.)

"Smokin'" Bert Cooper (PABHOF 2017) was an exciting puncher from Sharon Hill, Pennsylvania. He won the NABF and the Pennsylvania state titles as a cruiserweight before moving up to the heavyweight division. As a heavyweight, Cooper won another NABF title and lost a world title bid to Evander Holyfield in 1991. The following year, Cooper lost a memorable WBO title brawl with Michael Moorer. Cooper scored two knockdowns but lost in round five. At the end of his career (1984–2012), Cooper's record was 38-25 (31 KOs). He died at age 53 in 2019. (Photograph by Pete Goldfield.)

Tyrone "Butterfly" Crawley (PABHOF 2010) was a Philadelphia southpaw who fought 24 times (1980–1988), including wins over Robin Blake, Gene Hatcher, Anthony Murray, Ernest Bing, Al Cater, and Edwin Curet. In 1985, Crawley won the NABF lightweight title by decision over Charlie "Choo Choo" Brown. The 12-round win sent him directly into a WBA world title contest against champion Livingstone Bramble. Bramble retained the title by TKO in round 13. Crawley finished his career with a record of 22-2 (7 KOs). He later trained his son Tyrone Jr. Crawley died in 2021 at age 62. (Photograph by Pete Goldfield.)

Gus Dorazio (PABHOF 1973, right) was born Justine Vincolota in 1916 in Philadelphia. As an amateur, he won the Mid-Atlantic championship in 1935. Dorazio faced many top light heavyweights and heavyweights during his professional career (1935–1946). He defeated Harry Bobo, Bob Pastor, and Al McCoy before challenging heavyweight champion Joe Louis at home in Philadelphia in 1941. Louis (left) retained his title in two rounds. Dorazio compiled an overall record of 71-23-1 with one no contest and 19 KOs. He died at age 69 in 1986. (Author's collection.)

Forever in the shadow of his older brother Tyrone, Mike Everett (PABHOF 2010) had an excellent amateur career before launching a professional run in 1972. Victories over Norman Goins, Miguel Barreto, and Dale Hernandez helped him land a title shot against WBC junior welterweight champion Saensak Muangsurin in 1977. Under sweltering conditions in an outdoor ring in his homeland of Thailand, Muangsurin stopped Everett in six rounds to retain his title. Born in 1954, Everett finished fighting in 1979 with a 24-10-1 (11 KOs) record. (Author's collection.)

Gifted southpaw Tyrone Everett (PABHOF 2006) was shot and killed at age 24 in 1977, just six months after losing a highly controversial decision in a world title bout. On November 30, 1976, Alfredo Escalera retained his WBC junior lightweight championship with an outrageous 15-round decision over "The Mean Machine" at the Spectrum. It was Everett's only professional defeat in 37 bouts. Everett won both the USBA and NABF regional titles during his career (1971–1977). (Author's collection.)

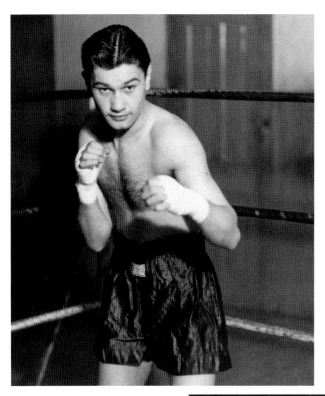

Southpaw Tommy Forte (PABHOF 2000) defeated reigning bantamweight champion Lou Salica in a 10-round nontitle bout in 1940. The upset instigated a rematch the following year with the championship on the line. Salica retained his crown with a narrow decision. Five months later, Salica defended the title again with an easier 15-round win against Forte. All three fights were in Philadelphia. Forte retired in 1947 (his career began in 1936) with a record of 43-14-2, one no contest, and 20 KOs. He died in 2001 at age 82. (Author's collection.)

Marvis Frazier (PABHOF 1998, right), son of former heavyweight champion Joe Frazier, had large shoes to fill. He won the first 10 bouts of his career (1980–1988), including victories over Steve Zouski (left), James Broad, and Joe Bugner. However, when rushed into a world title contest against Larry Holmes, Frazier, born in 1960, fell in the first round. He rebounded with wins over Bernard Benton, James Tillis, Jose Ribalta, and "Bonecrusher" Smith but lost against a rising Mike Tyson in 1986 in another first-round knockout. Frazier won his last three fights and retired with a record of 19-2 (8 KOs). (Author's collection.)

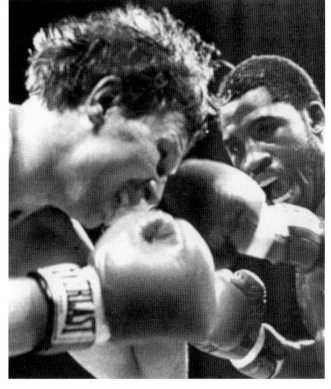

Tony "Dynamite" Green (PABHOF 2018, left) won the Pennsylvania featherweight title with a 10th-round TKO of Myron Taylor in 1991. Other key victories against Julian Solis, Fernando Rodriguez, Tommy Barnes, Enrique Sanchez, and Rudy Zavala helped earn him an opportunity to fight Alejandro Gonzalez for the WBC world featherweight championship in 1995. Green, born in 1966, lost by TKO in nine rounds. He retired in 1996 with a record of 23-6-1 (15 KOs). He is pictured with his uncle and manager/trainer Dave Wilkes. (Photograph by Pete Goldfield.)

Hard-punching Earl "The Pearl" Hargrove (PABHOF 2014) scored 24 consecutive knockouts to open his 38-bout career (1979–1995). The streak led Hargrove to a 1984 fight for the vacant IBF junior middleweight title against Mark Medal in Atlantic City. Hargrove, born in 1956, started quickly, but Medal rallied to stop him in the fifth round. Hargrove went 5-4 in his last nine bouts and retired with a record of 32-6 (28 KOs). (Photograph by Pete Goldfield.)

Stanley "Kitten" Hayward (PABHOF 1986) was an attraction in Philadelphia, New York, and Europe from 1959 to 1977. He defeated Curtis Cokes, Bennie Briscoe, Percy Manning, Dick Turner, Vince Shomo, Tito Marshall, and Emile Griffith. He earned a title shot against Freddie Little for the vacant junior middleweight championship in 1969, which Little won by 15-round decision. Hayward fought another eight years and hung up his gloves with a record of 32-12-4 (18 KOs). He died in 2021 at age 82. (Author's collection.)

Richie Kates (PABHOF 2011) was a top contender in one of the richest eras of the light heavyweight division. In 1976, a bloody Kates lost by heartbreaking final-round TKO to WBA champion Victor Galindez. In the rematch the following year, Galindez retained his title by decision. However, Kates's career (1970–1983) also included a North American championship and key bouts against Len Hutchins, Roger Russell, Pierre Fourie, Matthew Saad Muhammad, and James Scott. Kates retired with a record of 44-6 (23 KOs). He died in 2023 at age 69. (Peltz Boxing Promotions.)

WORLD TITLE CHALLENGERS

Teon Kennedy (PABHOF 2023), born in 1986, won a national amateur championship before winning two regional titles and earning a world title shot as a professional junior featherweight (2007–2013). He won the USBA belt in 2009 with a TKO over Francisco Rodriguez and won the NABF title in 2010 by stopping Alex Becerra. His best win came against Jorge Diaz in 2011. The following year, Kennedy challenged Guillermo Rigondeaux for the WBA world title but lost in five rounds. He closed his career with a 19-2-2 (7 KOs) record. (Photograph by John DiSanto.)

Boston-born Danny Kramer (PABHOF 2017) was a left-handed Philadelphia featherweight with 184 professional bouts from 1917 to 1930. He reached the fourth spot in *The Ring* rankings during the mid-1920s and scored victories over Mike Dundee, Abe Friedman, Jimmy Mendo, and Alex Hart. Kramer faced Louis "Kid" Kaplan in 1925 for the vacant world 126-pound championship at Madison Square Garden in New York City. Kaplan stopped Kramer in round nine to win the title. Kramer died in 1971 at age 70. (Author's collection.)

Marvin Mack (PABHOF 2018) won the WBC Continental Americas light heavyweight title with an 11th-round knockout of Lawrence Carter in 1986. Later the same year, he challenged IBF super middleweight world champion Chong Pal Park in Japan. The champion successfully defended the title with a 15-round decision. During his eight years in the ring (1982–1990), Mack, born in 1961, also faced Bobby Czyz, Kelvin Kelly, Frank Tate, and James Kinchen. He closed out his career with a record of 18-8-1 (10 KOs). (Photograph by Pete Goldfield.)

Yusaf Mack (PABHOF 2023) vied for the world title in two weight divisions during his 31-8-2 (17 KOs) career from 2000 to 2014. In 2011, Mack, born in 1980, lost to IBF light heavyweight champion Tavoris Cloud in his first world title opportunity. The following year, he lost a bid to IBF world super middleweight champion Carl Froch. However, "The Mack Attack" won regional titles at super middleweight (USBA) and light heavyweight (NABF, USBA, and UBA) as well as the Pennsylvania light heavyweight championship. (Photograph by John DiSanto.)

Born in Antigua, Jerry "The Bull" Martin (PABHOF 2011) attempted to win the world light heavyweight championship three times during his career (1976–1984). In 1980, he lost to WBA champion Eddie Mustafa Muhammad. In 1981, Martin was stopped by WBC champion Matthew Saad Muhammad. In his next bout, Martin lost to WBC champion Dwight Muhammad Qawi in 1982. Earlier, Martin won both the USBA and NABF regional titles and was the first to defeat James Scott at Rahway State Prison in New Jersey. Martin retired with a 25-7 (17 KOs) record. He died in 2021 at age 67. (Photograph by Pete Goldfield.)

Born Louis Massucci, Lew Massey (PABHOF 1975) fought 122 times, including wins over Bud Taylor, Harry Blitman, Tony Falco, Freddie Cochrane, Vic Burrone, Davey Adleman, and Midget Fox during his career, which spanned from 1928 to 1939. In 1931, Massey lost his chance at a world title when he was defeated by junior lightweight champion Benny Bass in a 10-round contest. Massey retired from the ring with a record of 72-41-9 (12 KOs). He died at age 82 in 1993. (Author's collection.)

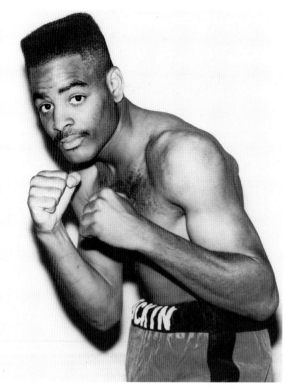

"Rockin' " Rodney Moore (PABHOF 2007) won the Pennsylvania junior welterweight title with a 12-round decision over Ali Saad Muhammad at the Blue Horizon. It was one of Moore's 22 appearances at the legendary Philadelphia venue. His three attempts at world titles were unsuccessful. He lost a 1993 title bout against Charles Murray. In 1994, WBA champion Frankie Randall defended his title against Moore. Finally, Moore, born in 1965, lost to welterweight champion Felix Trinidad in 1996. He quit the ring with a record of 38-10-2 (20 KOs). (Photograph by Pete Goldfield.)

Known as the "Pittsburgh Dentist," Frank Moran (PABHOF 2012) was a professional heavyweight with nearly 70 bouts between 1908 and 1922. He twice vied for the world heavyweight championship. In 1914, Moran lost a 20-round decision to champion Jack Johnson before 30,000 fans in Paris. Two years later, he lost his second try for the heavyweight crown, losing a 10-round decision to champion Jess Willard at Madison Square Garden. He died in 1967 at age 80. (Author's collection.)

FRANK MORAN

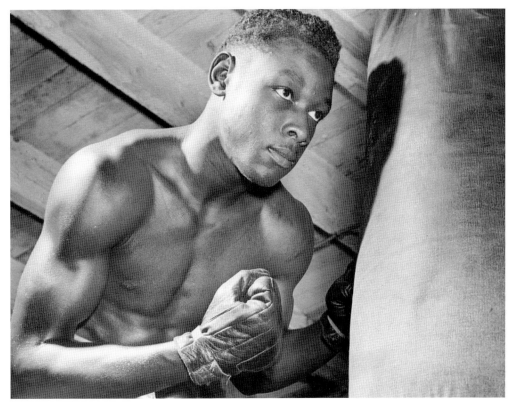

South Carolina–born Wesley Mouzon (PABHOF 1993) was a teenage lightweight sensation during his brief career (1944–1946). Mouzon beat experienced foes Eddie Giosa, Santa Bucca, and Jimmy Joyce and drew with NBA world champion Ike Williams in a 1945 nontitle bout while still in his teens. In 1946, Mouzon knocked out reigning world lightweight champion Bob Montgomery in another nontitle fight. In their championship rematch three months later, Montgomery knocked out Mouzon. Wesley retired immediately afterward with a detached retina. He had a 26-3-1 (10 KOs) record and was still just 19 years old. Mouzon had a second career as a trainer. He died in 2003 at age 75. (Author's collection.)

Born Alexander DeRenza, Battling Murray (PABHOF 2022) fought more than 150 times in his career (1915–1927). His opponents included Indian Russell, "Kid" Wolfe, "Battling" Harry Leonard, Patsy Wallace, and Jimmy Mendo. In 1920, Murray challenged Jimmy Wilde for the world flyweight championship. He knocked the champion down but lost by an eighth-round TKO. Murray was also once considered the American flyweight champion. He died in 1979 at age 79. (Author's collection.)

A veteran of 96 professional fights, Tommy O'Toole (PABHOF 1962) hated to box outside his hometown of Philadelphia, having only fought elsewhere five times. In 1909, O'Toole traveled to Boston and lost by decision to Abe Attell in a try for the world featherweight title. During his career (1904–1913), O'Toole won newspaper decisions against Attell, former world bantamweight champion Danny Dougherty, Ad Wolgast, Kid Beebe, Patsy Kline, Willie Gibbs, Harry Decker, and Tommy O'Keefe. He died in 1971 at age 84. (Author's collection.)

Zahir "Z-Man" Raheem (PABHOF 2022), a 1996 Olympian, won 25 straight bouts to start his professional career (1996–2014). He defeated Erik Morales by unanimous decision to win the vacant WBC International lightweight regional title. In his next bout, he challenged WBO world champion Acelino Frietas but lost a close split decision. Born in 1976, Raheem fought 10 more times, winning eight, including a bout to claim the vacant NABO junior welterweight regional title. He retired in 2014 with a record of 35-3 (21 KOs). (Photograph by Darryl Cobb Jr.)

Lightweight contender Ivan "Mighty" Robinson (PABHOF 2013) had an outstanding amateur career before turning professional in 1992. He took the USBA lightweight regional title against Demetrio Ceballos in 1995. The following year, Robinson, born in 1971, challenged IBF world champion Phillip Holiday, who retained the title by decision. In his highest-profile fights, Robinson beat Arturo Gatti twice. Their first fight was called the "1998 Fight of the Year" by *The Ring*. He finished in 2008 with a record of 32-12-2 (12 KOs). (Peltz Boxing Promotions.)

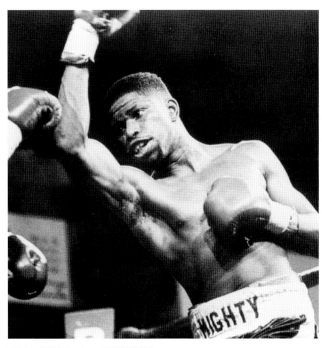

Ernie "Grog" Singletary (PABHOF 2018) fought 31 bouts over 10 years (1974–1984) before receiving a world title opportunity in the final fight of his career. Singletary, born in 1952, faced Murray Sutherland for the vacant IBF world super middleweight championship but lost the 15-round decision. He retired afterward with a record of 26-6 (8 KOs). He also faced Thomas Hearns, Alan Minter, and Frank Fletcher. (Author's collection.)

"Mighty" Myron Taylor (PABHOF 2020), Meldrick Taylor's older brother, was a national Golden Gloves champion as an amateur. In the professional ranks, he fought numerous contenders, including Bernard Taylor, Kenny Baysmore, and Lupe Suarez. These victories led to a world title fight against IBF featherweight champion Calvin Grove in 1988. Taylor lost the 15-round decision. Born in 1960, Taylor won a regional title (WBC Continental Americas) in 1989. He retired in 1991 with a record of 29-9-2 (16 KOs). (Photograph by Pete Goldfield.)

"The Punching Postman" Tony Thornton (PABHOF 2019) won a regional title at middleweight and earned three world title fights at super middleweight during his career (1983–1995). He lost by decision to WBO super middleweight champion Chris Eubank in 1992. He challenged James Toney for the IBF super middleweight title in 1993 but again lost a decision. Finally, in his last bout, Thornton fell to Roy Jones Jr. in round three of another fight for the IBF 168-pound crown. He retired with a record of 37-7-1 (26 KOs) and died in a motorcycle accident in 2009 at age 49. (Author's collection.)

Delaware's Dave Tiberi (PABHOF 2009) lost a highly controversial 1992 decision to IBF world middleweight champion James Toney in the final bout of his career, which began in 1985. Tiberi was so outraged by the scores of the official judges that he immediately retired from boxing in protest. Tiberi rejected lucrative rematch offers from Toney and left the sport for good with a record of 22-3-3 (7 KOs). Tiberi, born in 1966, made nine appearances in Pennsylvania and 15 in Atlantic City. (Photograph by Pete Goldfield.)

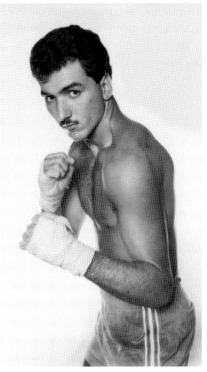

Welterweight Gil Turner (PABHOF 1967) won the first 31 bouts of his career (1950–1958), including victories over Ike Williams and Beau Jack. The streak earned Tuner a world title fight with Kid Gavilan in 1952. In a competitive fight, Gavilan won by TKO in 11 rounds before 39,025 fans in Philadelphia. Turner fought for another six years and appeared on national television many times but never earned another title opportunity. He retired with a 56-19-2 (35 KOs) record. Turner died in 1996 at age 65. (Author's collection.)

Born in Dawson, Alaska, Billy Wallace (PABHOF 2020) boxed professionally for 15 years beginning in 1920. He was a top-ranked fighter who had more than 170 bouts and was featured on the February 1928 cover of *The Ring*. He defeated Johnny Jadick, Billy Petrolle, Tommy Herman, Louis "Kid" Kaplan, Cuddy DeMarco, Joe Glick, and Bruce Flowers. In 1931, Wallace landed a title bout with NBA world champion Jack "Kid" Berg, losing the 10-round decision. He died at age 85 in 1986. (Author's collection.)

Slick heavyweight Jimmy Young (PABHOF 1998) gave Muhammad Ali a scare in their world heavyweight championship fight in 1976. Ali won the close decision, but many believed Young should have taken the title. Young beat top fighters, including George Foreman, Ron Lyle, and Jose Roman, during his up-and-down career (1969–1990). However, losses to Ken Norton, Earnie Shavers, Michael Dokes, Gerry Cooney, Greg Page, and Tony Tucker stalled the career of the once promising boxer (35-18-3, 11 KOs). He died in 2005 at age 56. (Author's collection.)

# 3

# STATE AND REGIONAL CHAMPIONS

Jerome Artis (PABHOF 2015) won a national amateur championship in 1972, defeating "Sugar" Ray Leonard in the quarter finals. As a professional, Artis started well, scoring impressive wins against Sammy Goss, Alfonso Evans, Johnny Copeland, Jose Fernandez, and "Red" Berry. However, after his TKO loss to Alexis Arguello, Artis declined. He accumulated many losses, yet still managed to win the Pennsylvania lightweight championship in 1980. He retired in 1987 with an even record, 27-27-4 (9 KOs), and died in 1999 at age 45. (Peltz Boxing Promotions.)

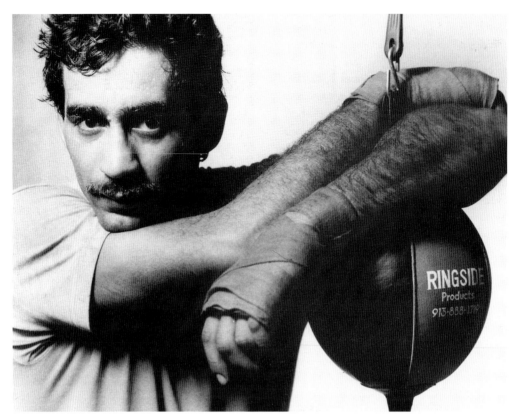

Bethlehem, Pennsylvania's Angel Cruz (PABHOF 2018) was born in 1956 in Puerto Rico but debuted as a professional in Allentown, Pennsylvania. During his career (1977–1988), Cruz scored wins over Alfredo Escalera and Saoul Mamby. He won the vacant New York state lightweight championship in 1984 with a victory over Ricky Young and defended the title twice. Losses to Howard Davis Jr., Vilomar Fernandez, and Charlie "White Lightning" Brown kept him from a world title fight. He retired in 1988 with a 27-6-2 (8 KOs) record. (Author's collection.)

Jimmy Deoria (PABHOF 2004, left) was a popular lightweight from Phoenixville, Pennsylvania, who campaigned in the professional ranks between 1990 and 1996. In 1993, he won the Pennsylvania state title with a TKO of Gene Reed. Deoria, born in 1970, continued to climb the ranks with wins over Charlie "White Lightning" Brown and Kelvin Seabrooks, but consecutive losses to Angel Manfredy, Charles Murray, and Ivan Robinson halted his rise. Deoria retired with a record of 20-7 (8 KOs). He is pictured with his father and assistant trainer Jim Deoria Sr. (PABHOF 2020). (Jimmy Deoria.)

Derek "Pooh" Ennis (PABHOF 2020) was the eldest brother of a fighting family from Philadelphia. He had a fine career as a junior middleweight between 2002 and 2014. Ennis, born in 1980, won the Pennsylvania state championship with a decision over Troy Browning in 2008. The following year, he earned the vacant USBA title with an action-packed decision over Eromosele Albert. Ennis defended this belt once, a 12-round decision over Gabriel Rosado in 2010. He closed his career with a record of 24-5-1 (13 KOs). (Photograph by John DiSanto.)

Slick southpaw Anthony "Two Guns" Fletcher (PABHOF 2018) was one of three fighting Fletcher brothers. His outstanding amateur career included a 1977 national championship. He made his professional debut in 1980 and went unbeaten in his first 22 bouts, including victories over Freddie Pendleton, Livingstone Bramble, and Sammy Goss. In 1989, he defeated Marvin Garris to take the Pennsylvania lightweight title. Born in 1957, Fletcher left the sport in 1990 after a criminal conviction with a record of 24-4-1 (8 KOs). (Photograph by Pete Goldfield.)

Southpaw Frank "The Animal" Fletcher (PABHOF 2018, right) was an exciting all-action brawler and the eldest of the Fletcher brothers. Many of his bouts (1976–1985) were wild, exciting affairs. He won the ESPN middleweight championship in 1980. The following year, Fletcher, born in 1954, earned the USBA title with a win over Norberto Sabatar. Fletcher defended this belt in memorable battles with Ernie Singletary, Tony Braxton, Clint Jackson, and James Green. Much of his 18-6-1 (12 KOs) career played out on national television. He is pictured with his trainer Elvin Thompson (PABHOF 2023). (Photograph by Pete Goldfield.)

The youngest of the fighting Fletcher brothers, Troy Fletcher (PABHOF 2021) captured the Pennsylvania bantamweight title in his 10th pro bout with a 12-round decision over Bryan Jones at the Blue Horizon in 1985. Fletcher, born in 1961, vied for the Pennsylvania featherweight title in 1992 against Fernando Rodriguez but lost a 12-round decision. The loss was the first of a nine-bout skid that ended Fletcher's career with a 13-10-2 (2 KOs) record. (Photograph by Pete Goldfield.)

"Machine Gun" Marvin Garris (PABHOF 2021) won the Pennsylvania lightweight title by 12-round decision over Victor Flores in 1985 at the Blue Horizon. He defended the title in 1986 by stopping Anthony Williams on cuts in seven rounds. In 1989, Garris lost his belt to Anthony Fletcher by decision. In between these state title fights, Garris, born in 1963, lost nontitle bouts to Micky Ward and Roger Mayweather. The loss to Fletcher was the final fight of his 15-10-1 (6 KOs) career. (Photograph by Pete Goldfield.)

Trenton, New Jersey, boxer Sammy Goss (PABHOF 2004) was a key figure in Pennsylvania, fighting often at the Spectrum, Blue Horizon, and Arena. He won the NABF featherweight title against Lloyd Marshall at the Spectrum in 1971 and defended it at Madison Square Garden against Walter Seeley. Born in 1947, Goss won the USBA junior lightweight championship by beating Jose Fernandez at New York's Felt Forum. Goss also defeated Edwin Viruet, Augie Pantellas, Luis Lopez, and Jose Luis Lopez. He retired in 1981 with a record of 43-15-3 (19 KOs). (Author's collection.)

Alfonso Hayman (PABHOF 2017), a tough and surly welterweight journeyman, was best remembered as the first man to go the distance with rising welterweight knockout artist Thomas Hearns (1979). In another career highlight, Hayman, born in 1948, won the Pennsylvania welterweight title by decision over Mario Saurennann in 1974. He also beat Johnny Gant, Roy Barrientos, and William Watson and fought to a spectacular draw with fellow Philadelphian "Youngblood" Williams in 1977. Hayman retired in 1980 with a 21-20-5 (12 KOs) record. (Author's collection.)

Vaughn "Turtle" Hooks (PABHOF 2019) fought a 10-year professional career (1983–1993) and won the Pennsylvania light heavyweight championship with a sixth-round TKO of Kelvin Kelly in 1987. In his next bout, he defeated Frankie Swindell by decision at Philadelphia's National Guard Armory to earn the USBA regional 175-pound title. However, when Hooks, born in 1969, failed a post-fight drug test, the result was changed to a no contest, and the title was immediately vacated. Hooks won four of his next six bouts and retired with a 19-2 record with 10 KOs and one no contest. (Photograph by Pete Goldfield.)

Philadelphia southpaw Hugh "Buttons" Kearney
(PABHOF 2016) won his first 17 bouts, including
a 1986 twelve-round decision over future
world champion Steve Little to win the vacant
Pennsylvania welterweight championship. He
also beat Milton Leaks and Darryl Anthony
and drew with Derwin Richards. However, after
losing two of his last three fights against Jorge
Maysonet and Vincent Pettway, Kearney, born in
1964, retired in 1988 with a record of 18-2-1 (5
KOs). (Photograph by Pete Goldfield.)

Kelvin "Special K" Kelly (PABHOF 2021) won both the ESPN and the Pennsylvania light
heavyweight championships during his career (1982–1987). He won the ESPN belt in 1985
by beating Freddie Guzman in Atlantic City. The following year, he took the state title with
a 12-round verdict over Lionel Byarm. Other significant victories came against Marvin Mack,
Everett Martin, and David Lee Royster. Kelly retired with a 14-3 (1 KO) record. Kelly, born in
1958, is pictured with his trainer, Marvin "Toochie" Gordon. (Photograph by Pete Goldfield.)

Thirty-eight bout professional "Irish" Billy Maher (PABHOF 1971) won the Pennsylvania lightweight championship in 1939 by 10-round decision against Tommy Speigal at the Philadelphia Arena. Speigal took the title with a 12-round decision two months later. Other key bouts for Maher included wins over Billy Arnold, Jackie Sheppard, Eddie Zivic, Jimmy Tygh, and Tony Morgano. After nine years in the ring (1937–1946), Maher quit with a record of 27-9-2 (9 KOs). He died in 2001 at age 85. (Author's collection.)

Arkansas-born Leotis Martin (PABHOF 2010) was a hard-luck heavyweight who scored impressive wins over Von Clay, Karl Mildenberger, Thad Spencer, and Don Warner during a seven-year career (1962–1969). His knockout of Sonny Banks was marred when Banks died of injuries sustained in the fight. His career highlight, a shocking 1969 knockout of Sonny Liston, earned him the NABF heavyweight title. However, shortly after the win, Martin was forced to retire due to a detached retina. His final record was 31-5 (19 KOs). He died in 1995 at age 56. (Author's collection.)

STATE AND REGIONAL CHAMPIONS

Nicknamed "Pound for Pound," Tony Martin (PABHOF 2015) won the NABF welterweight championship in 1996 with a 10th-round TKO of Kip Diggs. He defended the title twice against Diggs and Skipper Kelp. Earlier, Martin defeated former champions Charlie "Choo Choo" Brown and Livingstone Bramble as well as popular contender Micky Ward. In his final bout, Martin lost a 10-round decision against legend Julio Cesar Chavez in a 1997 nontitle fight. Tony retired with a record of 34-6-1 (12 KOs) and died in 2013 at age 52. (Photograph by Pete Goldfield.)

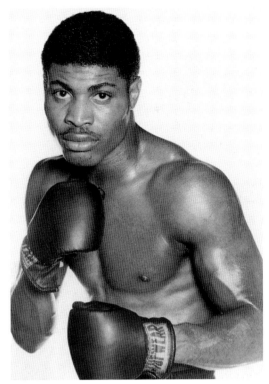

"Pittsburgh" Johnny Morris (PABHOF 2018, right) was a respected middleweight boxer with a quick jab and fast feet. During his career (1956–1968), Morris won the Pennsylvania state championship in 1960 with a decision over Jimmy Beecham. He defended against Al Avant and George Benton before losing the title to Benton in 1963. He also faced Joey Giardello and Jimmy Ellis. Morris lost to Luis Rodriguez but beat Rubin Carter and Jesse Smith before retiring with a record of 27-11 (16 KOs). Morris died in 2005 at age 66. He is pictured here against Billy Pickett. (Author's collection.)

Born in Philadelphia in 1943, Jack "The Giant" O'Halloran (PABHOF 2019) faced many important fighters during his boxing career (1966–1974), including George Foreman, Ken Norton, Ron Lyle, Joe Bugner, and Mac Foster. The best wins on his 34-21-2 (17 KOs) record came against Cleveland Williams, Terry Daniels, and Mando Ramos. In 1973, O'Halloran beat Charlie Reno to win the California heavyweight title. After he retired, O'Halloran acted in movies, including *Superman*, *Superman II*, and *King Kong*. (Author's collection.)

After winning a national amateur title in 1977, Curtis Parker (PABHOF 2008) won his first 17 professional bouts, including victories over Willie Monroe, Elisha Obed, Willie Warren, Mike Colbert, and David Love. His 1980 win against Love earned Parker the USBA middleweight belt. However, consecutive losses to Dwight Davidson, Mustafa Hamsho, and Wilford Scypion prevented Parker from receiving a world title shot. Born in 1959, Parker beat Tony Braxton, Frank Fletcher, and Ricky Stackhouse before his 29-9 (21 KOs) career ended in 1988. (Author's collection.)

STATE AND REGIONAL CHAMPIONS

Lancaster, Pennsylvania, southpaw Fernando Rodriguez (PABHOF 2021) was a two-time national Golden Gloves champion as an amateur. He made his professional debut in 1989 and fought 24 bouts through 1995. He won the Pennsylvania featherweight title by defeating Troy Fletcher over 12 rounds in 1992. He defended this title once against Tommy Barnes in 1993. In 1994 and 1995, Rodriguez, born in 1966, lost consecutive fights to Harrold Warren and Wilfredo Ruiz and retired with a record of 20-3-1 (9 KOs). (Photograph by Pete Goldfield.)

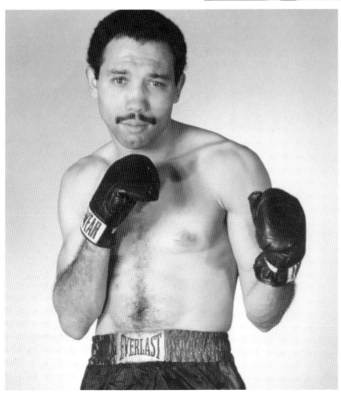

Born in Harlem, New York, Mario "Spider" Saurennann (PABHOF 2013) won a junior national 132-pound amateur championship in 1961. As a professional, fighting out of Philadelphia, Saurennann won the Pennsylvania welterweight title with a 12th-round TKO of C.L. Lewis at the Blue Horizon in 1971. He kept the title for three years. Born in 1943, Saurennann also defeated Bud Anderson and William Watson and drew with Art Kettles during his 13-year career (1965–1978) that ended with a 20-21-7 (6 KOs) record. (Author's collection.)

Charley Scott (PABHOF 2009) was an exciting fighter who reached the number one spot in the welterweight rankings in 1959. Scott's streaky career (1953–1966) included fights with Gil Turner, Luis Rodriguez, Benny Paret, Virgil Atkins, Gaspar Ortega, and Bennie Briscoe. In 1959, he beat Isaac Logart, Ralph Dupas, and, in his biggest win, Garnet Hart (for the Pennsylvania state title). The run pushed him to the top spot in the world rankings. Scott retired in 1966 with a record of 35-32 (20 KOs). He died in 1994 at age 57. (Peltz Boxing Promotions.)

James "Black Gold" Shuler (PABHOF year uncertain) was an outstanding amateur who missed his opportunity to go to the Olympics when the United States boycotted the 1980 games. As a professional (1980–1986), Shuler won his first 22 bouts, including a 1982 decision over "Sugar" Ray Seales to earn the NABF middleweight title. He defended the title twice against contenders Clint Jackson and James Kinchen. In 1986, he lost his belt to Thomas Hearns by knockout. One week later, Shuler died in a motorcycle accident at age 26. His final record was 22-1 (16 KOs). (Author's collection.)

Born Edward Smyth in Philadelphia, "Gunboat" Smith (PABHOF 2014) fought nearly 150 professional bouts between 1909 and 1921. He faced the best boxers of his era, including Jack Dempsey, Harry Greb, Jess Willard, Harry Wills, Jack Blackburn, Battling Levinsky, Sam Langford, Frank Moran, Kid Norfolk, Georges Carpentier, and Jack Dillon. While Jack Johnson was world champion, Smith won the "White Heavyweight Championship of the World" in 1914. Early in his career, he also won the US Army-Navy heavyweight championship. Smith died in 1974 at age 87. (Author's collection.)

Born in Florida, Jimmie Sykes (PABHOF 2007) lived in and fought out of Philadelphia. His 13-year professional campaign (1971–1984) included wins over Tony Tassone and Bennie Briscoe in the legend's final bout. Sykes's best victory was a major upset against undefeated prospect Steve Traitz Jr. in 1983. Sykes knocked out the 16-0 Traitz in round four at the Spectrum to win the Pennsylvania middleweight championship. It was the most memorable moment of his 13-11-1 (9 KOs) career. He died in 2020 at age 66. (Photograph by Pete Goldfield.)

The older brother of two-time heavyweight champion Tim Witherspoon, Anthony Witherspoon (PABHOF 2015) won both the Pennsylvania light heavyweight title and the WBA Americas cruiserweight championship during his nine-year career (1981–1990). The state championship came in 1987 with a stoppage of Al Shoffner in round seven. Two years later, Witherspoon took the regional title with a 12-round decision over Bash Ali. Born in 1955, Anthony lost his final two bouts and retired with a 19-7 (13 KOs) record. (Photograph by Pete Goldfield.)

Born Henry Grayo, Henry "Kid" Wolfe (PABHOF 1977) was a professional flyweight with nearly 60 bouts from 1918 to 1933. In 1924, he won the Pennsylvania state championship with a 10-round decision over Bobby Burke at the Reading Armory. Wolfe also beat Battling Murray, Benny Schwartz, Marty Gold, Sammy Novia, and Young Dencio. He lost to future world champions Pancho Villa and Frankie Genaro in official contests. In 1977, Wolfe died at age 79, one month after his induction into the PABHOF. (Author's collection.)

# 4

# LOCAL HEROES

Sidney "Sweet Pea" Adams (PABHOF 2009) won a national junior amateur championship in 1957. As a professional (1958–1962), he won 15 of his first 17 bouts, including victories over Brown Lee, Bobby Rogers, and Jethro Cason. In 1960, he rushed into a match with 69-bout veteran Kenny Lane and lost in one round. Adams went on to defeat Willie Stevenson and J.D. Ellis before retiring with a record of 17-5-2 (9 KOs). Adams died in 2020 at age 84. (Photograph by Jim Rogge.)

Billy Arnold (PABHOF 2010, right) was a teenage phenomenon who, while still in high school, raced up the welterweight rankings during the 1940s. Arnold went unbeaten in his first 30 bouts before losing to 192-fight veteran and former champion Fritzie Zivic (left) at Madison Square Garden in 1945. He lost to Rocky Graziano in his next bout. Arnold went 12-7 in his final chapter and retired with a record of 41-9-1 (34 KOs). He died at age 68 in 1995. (Author's collection.)

Pittsburgh-based heavyweight Bob Baker (PABHOF 2016) won both the Intercity Golden Gloves and the New York Golden Gloves as an amateur in 1949. His professional career (1949–1959) opened with a 25-bout winning streak that included victories over Jimmy Bivins, Marty Marshall, and Sid Peaks. Although he was rated second in the world during the 1950s, Baker never received a world title shot. He retired with a record of 51-16-1 (20 KOs) and died at age 75 in 2002. (Author's collection.)

LOCAL HEROES

Joe Belfiore (PABHOF 1986) was a lightweight with 61 professional bouts (1941–1950). His 38-17-5, 18 KOs, and one no decision record included wins against Ernie Petrone, Fred D'Amico, and George "Dusty" Brown. Belfiore won 24 of his first 27 bouts and later had five 10-rounders against Orlando Zulueta, Willie Beltram, Terry Young, Johnny LaRusso, and Dion Bleta. After his fighting career, Belfiore was a trainer at South Philadelphia's Juniper Gym. Belfiore died in 2014 at age 81. (Author's collection.)

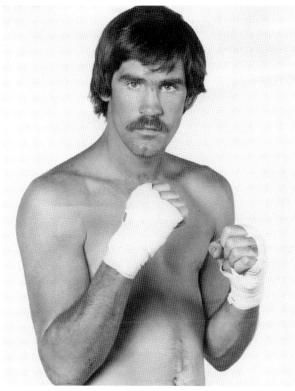

Richie "The Bandit" Bennett (PABHOF 2017) was a popular Upper Darby, Pennsylvania, middleweight between 1976 and 1983. In 1980, he split two 10-round main events with Bennie Briscoe in the biggest bouts of his career. He defeated Archie Andrews, Dan Snyder, and Bob Patterson. Bennett often fought in his hometown at the 69th Street Forum where he was a major attraction. Bennett's overall record was 25-6-2 (18 KOs). He died in 1991 at age 32. (Author's collection.)

"Handsome" Harry Blitman (PABHOF 1978) was a national amateur champion and professional contender with 78 professional fights (1926–1934). In 1928, Blitman defeated world featherweight champion Tony Canzoneri in a nontitle bout. Later that year, he lost to former world champion Benny Bass in a two-way slugfest. It was Blitman's first defeat and derailed a possible rematch with Canzoneri. He also faced Lew Massey, Tony Falco, and Midget Fox. Blitman died in 1972 at age 62. (Author's collection.)

Hard-hitting Pittsburgh-based heavyweight Harry Bobo (PABHOF 2016) was known as the "Peabody Paralyzer." He scored 24 knockouts during his career (1939–1944) and scored wins over Gus Dorazio, Nick Fiorentino, and Al Hart. While Joe Louis served in the US Army, Bobo won two versions of the Duration heavyweight championship. He lost both titles to Lee Q. Murray in 1943. The following year, blinded by an eye injury, Bobo retired with a record of 35-9. He died at age 46 in 1966. (Author's collection.)

Anthony "TKO" Boyle (PABHOF 2002) was a wildly popular local lightweight who battled 33 times over 10 years (1985–1995), mostly in Philadelphia and Atlantic City boxing rings. In his best victory, he defeated Johnny Carter by decision in 1988. Boyle, born in 1965, vied for regional titles four times but lost to Frankie Mitchell, Carl Griffith, Marty Jakubowski, and John Lark. He closed his professional career with a record of 26-6-1 (12 KOs). As an amateur, Boyle was a 1984 Philadelphia Golden Gloves champion. (Photograph by Pete Goldfield.)

Henry "Toothpick" Brown (PABHOF 2009) was a Philadelphia Diamond Belt champion as an amateur before turning professional in 1951. He defeated local talent, including Art Mullins, Tommy Reed, and Leslie Petway, and battled Boland Abrams in a deadlocked three-fight series. Brown, born in 1933, made eight appearances at Madison Square Garden. In 1956, he was on the brink of title contention when he knocked out L.C. Morgan on national television. However, he lost his next five bouts by knockout and retired with a 24-8-2 (14 KOs) record in 1958. (Author's collection.)

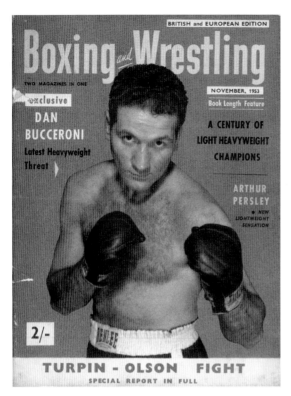

Dan "Butcher Boy" Bucceroni (PABHOF 1979), a heavyweight contender from 1947 to 1954, reached the number two spot in the world rankings. However, his hopes to fight champion Rocky Marciano were dashed when he lost by knockout to Tommy "Hurricane" Jackson in 1954. Bucceroni lost his next two bouts and retired 50-6 (34 KOs). Earlier, Bucceroni won fights against Rocky Jones, Roland LaStarza, and Freddie Beshore. He died in 2008 at age 80. (Author's collection.)

Born Francis DeVicaris, Frankie Caris (PABHOF 1976) fought 51 times and was once ranked in the top 30 as a light heavyweight by *The Ring*. He began his career (1933–1939) as a lightweight but fought as heavy as the 175-pound division. He defeated local talent Frankie Blair, Speedy Duval, and Roxie Forgione. In 1936, Caris drew with future light heavyweight champion Gus Lesnevich but lost the immediate rematch by decision. Caris also lost twice to Paul Pirrone. Caris retired with a 40-7-4 (5 KOs) record and died in 1987 at age 73. (Author's collection.)

One of three fighting brothers, Frankie Carto (PABHOF 1980, left) cracked *The Ring* top-10 featherweight rankings in 1946. His career (1941–1946) included wins over Johnny Aiello, Frankie Donato, Jackie Floyd, and Willie Weasel and losses against Lulu Constantino, Chalky Wright, Eddie Giosa, Phil Terranova, and Billy Graham. As an amateur, Carto was the 1939 and 1940 Philadelphia Golden Gloves champion and the 1941 Diamond Belt champion. He retired with a 41-13-3 (21 KOs) record. He died in 2005 at age 82. Carto is shown with Mike Evans (PABHOF 1976, center), and Johnny Forte (PABHOF 2020). (Author's collection.)

The youngest of the three fighting Carto brothers, Nunzio Carto (PABHOF 1982) was an outstanding amateur who won four major championships between 1944 and 1946. His 29-bout professional career (1946–1948) resulted in a 27-2 (13 KOs) record and included two decision wins over Willie Alexander. After retiring from the ring, he founded Carto Funeral Home in South Philadelphia, where he served as funeral director for decades. Carto died at age 92 in 2020. (Author's collection.)

"The Pride of Tacony," Eddie Cool (PABHOF 1975), was a naturally gifted boxer who fought 142 professional fights from 1928 to 1939. In 1936, Cool defeated reigning lightweight champion Lou Ambers in a nontitle bout but was never granted a rematch with the championship on the line. Despite a distaste for training and a heavy drinking lifestyle, Cool's remarkable career (97-29-16, 15 KOs) included victories over Fritzie Zivic, Freddie Cochrane, Benny Bass, Johnny Jadick, Tony Falco, Tony Morgano, Dick Welsh, and Lew Massey. He died in 1947 at age 35. (Author's collection.)

Born Thomas Ellis in New Orleans, Tommy Cross (PABHOF 2006) was a lanky lightweight with 79 bouts (1934–1942). Cross used his slippery boxing skills and quick left jab to score notable wins over Midget Wolgast, Eddie Cool, Lew Massey, Tommy Speigal, Gene Gallotto, and Charley Gomer. His final record was 44-26-8 with 9 KOs and one no contest. As an amateur, Cross was a Golden Gloves champion. After being inducted by the spinoff Pennsylvania State Boxing Hall of Fame, Cross was absorbed by the PABHOF in 2006. He died in the 1980s. (Author's collection.)

LOCAL HEROES

Born Louis Molinari in Philadelphia, Willie Curry (PABHOF 1981) was a professional welterweight (1919–1929) who had most of his 46 bouts in Pennsylvania. He fought local talent, including Darby Casper, Mickey Papner, Right Cross, Meyer Grace, Reddy Holt, Danny Gordon, Joe Bashara, and Alex Bader. His career-best wins were knockouts of Sam Robideau in 1924 and Billy Jones in 1928. After retirement, Curry was a truck driver for 37 years. He died in 1983 at age 81. (Author's collection.)

Born Hugh Clavin in Philadelphia, Young Erne (PABHOF year uncertain) had 274 professional bouts (by some accounts more than 400) as a lightweight (1900–1917). Also known as "Yi Yi" Erne, he faced multiple world champions, including Abe Attell, Harry Lewis, George Lavigne, George Chip, and Jack Britton, as well as contenders Leach Cross, "Harlem" Tommy Murphy, Mike Gibbons, and "Packey" McFarland. Most of his contests were no decision bouts. He died in 1944 at age 59. (Author's collection.)

Al Ettore (PABHOF 2011) was a top-10 heavyweight during his 83-bout career (1930–1939). He faced seven world champions, beating Pete Latzo, James Braddock, "Jersey" Joe Walcott, and John Henry Lewis (in one of three meetings). He lost to champions Joe Louis, Tommy Loughran, and Maxie Rosenbloom. Other important wins came against Gus Dorazio, Leroy Haynes (three times), Willie Reddish, and Steve Dudas. Ettore, rated number three in 1936, finished his career with a record of 62-17-4 (20 KOs). He died in 1988 at age 74. (Author's collection.)

Born Matthew Evancich, Mike Evans (PABHOF 1976) won two local amateur titles before turning professional in 1936. He went unbeaten in his first 23 fights, including consecutive wins over Eddie Cool, Tommy Speigal, and Tommy Cross, which earned him a bout with Bob Montgomery for the vacant Pennsylvania lightweight championship in 1939. Montgomery won a close decision and knocked Evans out in their rematch. Later, Evans beat Honey Mellody and Charley Gomer and won two of three against "Slugger" White. He lost to "Sugar" Ray Robinson in 1941 and retired in 1944 with a record of 36-8-1 (3 KOs). Evans died in 1987 at age 74. (Author's collection.)

Lightweight Eddie Giosa (PABHOF 1979) had 106 professional fights (1943–1954) and was rated in the top 10 by *The Ring*. He defeated future champions Carmen Basilio and Percy Bassett, former champions Lew Jenkins and Bob Montgomery, and contenders Lulu Constantino and Maxie Shapiro. Giosa lost bouts with champions Willie Pep, Ike Williams, Sandy Saddler, Beau Jack, and Carmen Basilio. He posted an overall record of 68-29-9 (9 KOs) and died in 2007 at age 82. (Author's collection.)

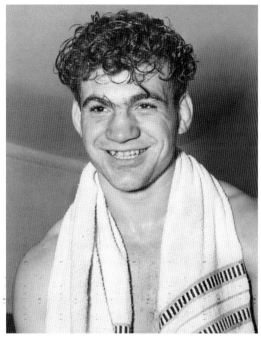

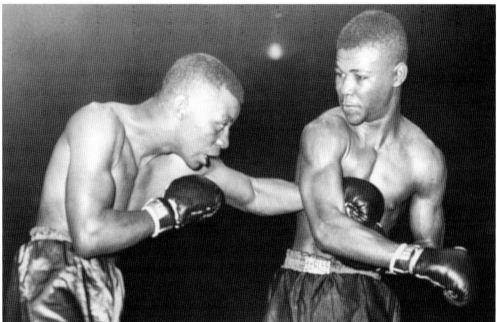

Otis Graham (PABHOF 2020, right) was a welterweight who fought many fine opponents in his 79-bout career (1945–1953). He lost to Joey Giardello, Bobo Olson, Kid Gavilan, Joey Giambra, Lee Sala, Walter Cartier, Paul Pender, and Dorsey Lay (left), but defeated Tommy Bell, "Honeychile" Johnson, Bernard Docusen, and Al Mobley. In 1950, Graham was ranked in the top 10 by *The Ring*. He retired in 1953 with a record of 40-33-6 (17 KOs). Graham died in 1968 at age 40. (Peltz Boxing Promotions.)

One of the most popular fighters of his era (1964–1968), "Gypsy" Joe Harris (PABHOF 2006, left) was a colorful showman with an unpredictable style. Harris defeated Stanley "Kitten" Hayward, Johnny Knight, Jose Stable, Dick DiVeronica, and world champion Curtis Cokes in a 1967 nontitle fight. Harris's only loss in 25 fights was against Emile Griffith (right). "Gypsy Joe" was forced to retire at age 22 when it was discovered that he was blind in his right eye. Harris, who appeared on the cover of *Sports Illustrated* in 1967, died in 1990 at age 44. (Author's collection.)

Hard-punching middleweight Eugene "Cyclone" Hart (PABHOF 2002) was a left hook specialist who scored 28 knockouts in his 30 victories (1969–1982). Born in 1952, Hart stopped his first 19 opponents, including Stanley Hayward, Leroy Roberts, and Vernon Mason. He was once ranked ninth by *The Ring*. However, losses to Marvelous Marvin Hagler, Willie Monroe, Bobby Watts, Eddie Mustafa Muhammad, and Vito Antuofermo cooled his rise in the ranks. His 1975 ten-round draw with Bennie Briscoe is considered a Philadelphia classic. (Peltz Boxing Promotions.)

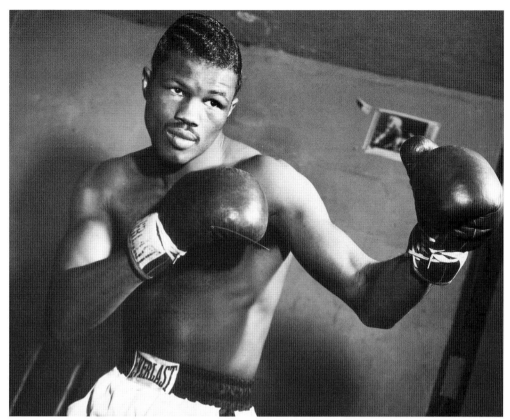

A national amateur champion in 1954, Garnet "Sugar" Hart (PABHOF 2009) was often compared to "Sugar" Ray Robinson early in his professional career (1954–1961). In the late 1950s, an eight-bout unbeaten streak against Gil Turner, Isaac Logart, Ralph Dupas, and Charley Cotton pushed Hart to the number-one spot in *The Ring* welterweight rankings. However, his savage crosstown war with Charley Scott for the Pennsylvania state championship ruined him as a fighter. Hart, with a 29-7-2 (22 KOs) record, died in 2003 at age 66. (Author's collection.)

"Smokin' " Wade Hinnant (PABHOF 2017) had a brief but impressive four-year career as a junior welterweight boxer (1975–1979). He was a rising prospect with victories over Mike Everett, Norman Goins, and Johnny Copeland when his career was cut short due to an eye injury. Hinnant, born in 1959, retired with a 14-2 (6 KOs) record. He eventually returned to the sport as a trainer, guiding Pennsylvania hall of famer Teon Kennedy to a world title fight in 2012. (Peltz Boxing Promotions.)

Kevin "The Spoiler" Howard (PABHOF 2006, left) will always be remembered best for knocking down "Sugar" Ray Leonard in their 1984 bout (pictured). Leonard rallied to win the fight by TKO, but Howard's legend was forged by this monumental career highlight. He won key fights against Dick Eklund, Bobby Joe Young, and Johnny Cooper during his career (1978–1986) and was ranked in the top 10 among welterweights. Born in 1960, he lost by decision to Marlon Starling for the USBA and NABF titles. (Author's collection.)

"Blackjack" Johnny Hutchinson (PABHOF 2006) had the misfortune of coming up during one of the most competitive eras of the lightweight division. He never won a world title but defeated good fighters like Sammy Angott, Jackie Sheppard, Bobby Ruffin, Tony Strazzeri, Augie Soliz, and Mike Belloise. However, his career was impeded by legends Ike Williams, Beau Jack, and Baby Arizmendi. Hutchinson's final record was 66-23-8 (30 KOs) during his career (1935–1944). He died in 1994 at age 76. (Author's collection.)

LOCAL HEROES

William "The Hammer" Jones (PABHOF 2017) was a hard-hitting welterweight from Philadelphia who knocked out 17 of his 23 opponents (21-2, 17 KOs) between 1989 and 1994. A Blue Horizon and Atlantic City favorite, Jones's TKO win over Willie Taylor at the Trump Plaza in Atlantic City was a memorable slugfest. Both fighters hit the canvas, but Jones won in round five. Jones, born in 1969, only lost to one fighter, Eric Holland, who beat him twice at the Blue Horizon. (Peltz Boxing Promotions.)

"Rabbit," Dorsey Lay (PABHOF 2012) was a promising lightweight prospect during his career (1942–1948). He defeated local rivals Otis Graham, Ellis Phillips, George LaRover, and Eddie Giosa and managed wins against out-of-towners Freddie Dawson, Gene Burton, Vince Dell'Orto, and "Dusty" Brown. However, he could not get past Ike Williams and Wesley Mouzon. Lay suffered an eye injury during his career and continued fighting until he went blind. He retired with a record of 40-18-1 (15 KOs) and died in 2016 at age 91. (Photograph by John DiSanto.)

Percy Manning (PABHOF 2014) was a welterweight prospect (1961–1969) who knocked out 10 of his first 11 opponents. However, Manning was limited by a fragile chin. All seven of his losses came by knockout against Dick Turner, "Kitten" Hayward, Bennie Briscoe (twice), Joe Shaw, Luis Rodriguez, and Charley Shipes. When he protected his chin, Manning beat Briscoe, Rodriguez, Jose Stable, Sidney Adams, and Billy Collins. He vied for the California state title in 1966 but was knocked out. Manning retired with a record of 17-7-1 (11 KOs) and died in 1979 at age 37. (Johnny Gilmore.)

Born in 1907, Mickey Martell (PABHOF 1990) was a welterweight from Philadelphia who fought 42 bouts between 1922 and 1931, including victories against Bobby Barrett, Danny Gordon, Abe Cohen, and Pat Haley. However, in the final 14 fights of his career, Martell only won once. He served in the US Army Air Corps during World War II and died in his 70s. His younger brother Richie Martell (PABHOF 1986) was a lightweight and welterweight boxer with 59 professional fights from 1924 to 1932. (Author's collection.)

LOCAL HEROES

Len Matthews (PABHOF 2007) was a sensational fighter who seemed destined for a world title. He defeated experienced boxers "Pappy" Gault, "Toothpick" Brown, Tommy Tibbs, Orlando Zulueta, and Ray Lancaster during his career (1957–1964). He was knocked out by future champion Carlos Ortiz in 1959 but later attained a number-one ranking after wins against Johnny Gonsalves, "Candy" McFarland, Lahouari Godih, and Kenny Lane. Matthews retired due to an eye injury at age 24. His final record was 42-10-3 (29 KOs). He died in 2005 at age 66. (Author's collection.)

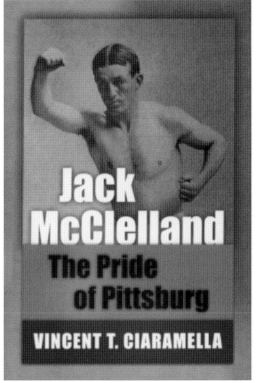

"The Pride of Pittsburgh," Jack McClelland (PABHOF 2020), fought 105 times as a featherweight (1896–1911). In his best win, McClelland defeated world champion Abe Attell by a 15-round decision in a 1904 over-the-weight nontitle fight. Afterward, McClelland was avoided by Attell and never fought for the championship. Other wins came against Tim Callahan, Tommy Sullivan, "Crocky" Boyle, Willie Fitzgerald, and Sammy Smith. McClelland died in 1954 at age 81. His great-great-grandson Vincent Ciaramella wrote a biography of the fighter in 2018. (Vincent Ciaramella.)

Born James Mangano, Jimmy Mendo (PABHOF 1968) began fighting at 17. His campaign as a bantamweight and featherweight included 88 professional bouts between 1918 and 1929. Mendo split two fights with Benny Bass, winning a newspaper decision over the future two-time champion in 1922 and losing by knockout in 1929, one month before Bass won his second world title. Mendo also faced Joe Lynch, Tod Morgan, Danny Kramer, and "Battling" Harry Leonard. He died in 1975 at age 75. (Author's collection.)

Willie "The Worm" Monroe (PABHOF 1990, left) was part of an outstanding group of Philadelphia middleweights during the 1970s. Monroe is best remembered for his clear-cut victory over a rising Marvelous Marvin Hagler in 1976. Hagler (right) won their two subsequent fights. Monroe also defeated "Cyclone" Hart, "Kitten" Hayward, Billy Douglas, Carlos Marks, Leroy Roberts, and Willie Warren. He was ranked third by *The Ring*. Monroe's complete record was 40-10-1 (26 KOs) during his career (1969–1981). He died in 2019 at age 73. (Author's collection.)

LOCAL HEROES

Brothers Pal Moore (PABHOF 1973), Willie Moore (PABHOF 2020), Reddy Moore (PABHOF 2023), and Frankie Moore were four of the five boxing Von Franzke brothers along with Al Moore (not pictured). Pal Moore was the most accomplished, with 135 bouts (1907-1922), including fights with six world champions. He died in 1943 at age 52. Willie Moore had 80 fights, including knockouts of Tommy Langdon and Young Jack O'Brien. He died in 1974 at age 80. Reddy Moore fought 68 times (1906-1926), including bouts with Jack Britton and Kid Beebe. Reddy died in 1961 at age 72. (Author's collection.)

Left-handed lightweight contender Tony Morgano (PABHOF 1965) beat many fine fighters in 72 bouts between 1929 and 1941, including former world champion Johnny Jadick, Freddie Cochrane, Bruce Flowers, Eddie Cool, Harry Blitman, Eddie Shea, Lew Feldman, Midget Fox, Matty White, and Ernie Caesar. After his retirement from the ring, Morgano ran the Southside Boys Club gym in South Philadelphia and served as president of the VBA-Ring One for 20 years (1964-1984). He died in 1985 at age 71. (Author's collection.)

Welterweight Mayon Padlo (PABHOF 1993) fought 103 times between 1937 and 1952. He defeated former champion Midget Wolgast but lost to former champion Fritzie Zivic and future champions Bob Montgomery and Ike Williams. Other wins came against Milo Theodorescu, Saverio Turiello, Frankie Saia, and Gene Gollotto. In the February 1943 issue of *The Ring*, Padlo was ranked number 44 in the annual ratings. He posted a final record of 77-21-3 with 36 KOs and two no contests. He died in 2001 at age 92. (Author's collection.)

"The Broomall Bomber," Augie Pantellas (PABHOF 2001), was a popular junior lightweight who fought 32 of his 34 bouts in Pennsylvania (1967–1979). The hard-punching action fighter's career played out in two chapters. He went 22-5 through 1971 before pausing to battle drug addiction. In 1977, Pantellas returned for a seven-fight stretch. In this second chapter, Pantellas, born in 1944, defeated Sammy Goss and Robert Quintanilla but was knocked out by Bobby Chacon. He retired with a record of 28-6 (20 KOs). (Author's collection.)

LOCAL HEROES

Andre "Thee" Prophet (PABHOF 2016) was a brilliant prospect who knocked out 10 of 13 opponents in a very brief one-year career (1987–1988). After beating Nestor Flores, William Morris, Dawud Shaw, and David Nall, Prophet was killed in a motorcycle accident at age 20. The hit-and-run accident occurred two weeks after his 1988 knockout of Melvin Ricks. Prophet's manager, Scott Kendall, believed Andre would eventually grow into the heavyweight division and challenge Mike Tyson for the title. (Photograph by Pete Goldfield.)

Roger Russell (PABHOF 2015) won a national amateur championship in 1965 as a light heavyweight. His professional career (1965–1978) was promising until he began fighting much larger men at heavyweight. Despite wins over Leotis Martin and Lou Esa and a draw with Zora Folley, Russell fell victim to a long list of strong heavyweights, including Floyd Patterson, George Foreman, Roy Williams, and Mac Foster. He ended his career with a modest 12-18-2 record. Russell died in 2022 at age 75. (Author's collection.)

BABE RUTH
PHILADELPHIA'S
FEATHERWEIGHT
STAR

Antonio Scattino was a professional featherweight and lightweight boxer who fought 60 bouts from 1922 to 1931 using the ring name Babe Ruth (PABHOF 1978) at a time when baseball's famous "Bambino" was the biggest sports hero in the country. Ruth the boxer scored his best wins against Red Chapman, Billy Petrolle, Willie Patterson, Tommy Farley, Harry Ross, and Bobby Garcia. In 1922, Ruth faced a fighter named Ty Cobb (Samuel Kolb). Ruth died in 1971 at age 66. (Author's collection.)

Donora, Pennsylvania, middleweight Lee Sala (PABHOF 2017) was rated in the top 10 for five of the seven years he fought professionally (1946–1953). Sala defeated Otis Graham, Garth Panter, Charley Williams, Norman Hayes, Charley Zivic, and Joe Rindone. Losses to Tony DeMicco, Gene Hairston, Joey DeJohn, Billy Kilgore, and Bobo Olson interrupted lengthy winning stretches and kept Sala from a title shot. He retired with a 76-7 (48 KOs) record and died in 2012 at age 85. (Author's collection.)

Born James Roberts, Curtis "Hatchetman" Sheppard (PABHOF 2020) was a feared puncher during his heavyweight career (1938–1949). He was the only man to ever knock out Joey Maxim, and stopped 34 opponents overall. Sheppard, once ranked number two by *The Ring*, also beat Gus Dorazio, "Big Boy" Brown, Al Hart, Buddy Walker, and Lee Q. Murray. Sheppard lost to Archie Moore, "Jersey" Joe Walcott, Jimmy Bivins, and Melio Bettina. His final record was 52-33, 34 KOs, one no decision, and two no contests. He died in 1984 at age 63. (Author's collection.)

"Crazy Horse" Jesse Smith (PABHOF 2012) was a Philadelphia middleweight who clashed with Joey Giardello (twice), Henry Hank, Luis Rodriguez, and George Benton in a 63-bout career between 1953 and 1966. Impressive winning streaks pushed Smith into the top-10 rankings during the early 1960s. His best victories came against Ernest Burford, Jimmy Beecham, Mel Collins, Clarence Alford, and Gomeo Brennan. He retired with a 46-12-5 (33 KOs) record after losing a decision to Johnny Morris. He died in 2012 at age 78. (Author's collection.)

Frankie Sodano (PABHOF 1991) won a national amateur championship before representing the United States at the 1948 London Olympics. His professional career (1948–1954) included a fight with future champion Percy Bassett in 1952. Sodano's loss in this bout interrupted a 36-bout unbeaten streak that included victories over Bobby Bell, "Pappy" Gault, Bill Bossio (PABHOF 2020), Willie Alexander, Archie Devino, and Hermie Freeman. He closed his career with a record of 50-8-1 (22 KOs) and died in 2015 at age 84. (Author's collection.)

James Bark, one of Philadelphia's most popular fighters, fought under the name Jimmy Soo (PABHOF 1994). A lightweight of Irish and Chinese heritage, Soo (his grandfather's name) delighted fans with an action-packed, hard-hitting style. He won his first 34 bouts, including 20 by knockout. Soo's best wins came against Ray Lancaster, Earl Clemons, Tony Spano, Baby Ray Jones, and Charlie Cummings. After eight years (1953–1961), Soo retired with a 42-4 (24 KOs) record. He died in 2003 at age 70. (Author's collection.)

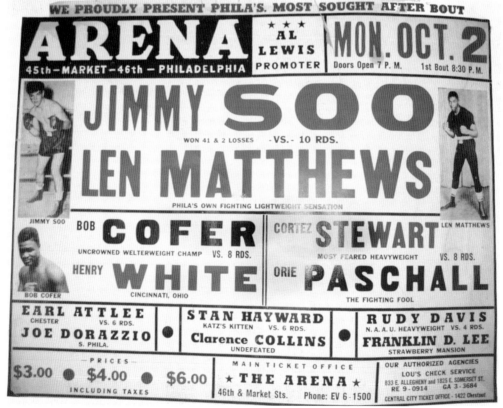

Although he had 54 professional bouts (1940–1945) and beat Harry Jeffra, Johnny Forte, Georgie Pace, and Spider Armstrong, Billy Speary's (PABHOF 1976) greatest moments came as an amateur. Born and raised in Nanticoke, Pennsylvania, Speary fought 198 amateur fights and won numerous championships. Between 1937 and 1939, he dominated the flyweight and bantamweight divisions, winning three national championships and three Intercity Golden Gloves titles. He lost 15 times as an amateur but avenged every defeat. Speary died in 1967 at age 49. (Author's collection.)

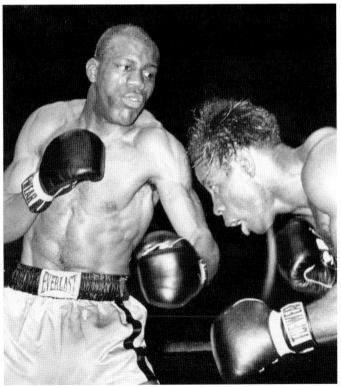

Dick Turner (PABHOF 2007, left) was a welterweight prospect who reached the number-five spot in *The Ring* rankings before his career was cut short by a detached retina. His 22 bouts (1959–1964) included upsets over Al Styles, Federico Thompson, and Isaac Logart (right). He suffered an eye injury in one of his final two bouts (losses to Jose Stable and "Kitten" Hayward) and retired with a 19-2-1 (11 KOs) record. Turner later helped guide nephews Frank, Anthony, and Troy Fletcher and trained boxers until his death at age 82 in 2020. (Author's collection.)

Jimmy Tygh (PABHOF 2014) boxed between 1937 and 1941. He went unbeaten in his first 27 bouts, including victories over Gene Gallotto, Jackie Sheppard, Bobby Green, and Billy Passan. He lost for the first time to Billy Maher but avenged the defeat with a 10-round decision two fights later. He also beat former champions Tony Canzoneri and Benny Bass and was a top-10 lightweight in 1940. After 71 bouts (1937–1941), Tygh retired with a record of 48-18-5 (9 KOs). He died in 1988 at age 71. (Author's collection.)

Bobby "Boogaloo" Watts (PABHOF 2004) was a third-ranked middleweight contender. He was the first man to beat Marvelous Marvin Hagler and defeated Willie Monroe, "Cyclone" Hart, Manuel Gonzalez, and Willie Warren during his 14-year career (1969–1983). Losses to David Love, Mustafa Hamsho, and Hagler (in a rematch) weakened his standing in the middleweight division rankings. After retiring with a 39-7-1 (22 KOs) record, Watts, born in 1949, trained a number of boxers, including Charles Brewer, Buster Drayton, and Rogers Mtagwa. (Photograph by Pete Goldfield.)

LOCAL HEROES

John DiMatteo fought 109 times in the flyweight and bantamweight divisions from 1925 to 1937 as Dick Welsh (PABHOF 2022). The quick-footed counterpuncher faced eventual world champions Midget Wolgast and Lou Salica as well as many top contenders. He beat Eddie Cool, Benny Goldstein, and Benny Schwartz. Welsh was ranked number nine in the world by the National Boxing Association and reached the number-five spot in *The Ring* as a bantamweight. He died in 1952 at age 43. (Author's collection.)

Ike White (PABHOF 2000) had a streaky middleweight career (1950–1969) against stiff competition, including Jose Torres, Bennie Briscoe, "Kitten" Hayward, Holly Mims, Joey Giambra, and Jimmy Beecham. He never won more than three bouts in a row and retired with a losing record (19-40-4, 4 KOs). However, White was a rugged fighter with wins over Boland Abrams, Mel Collins, and Johnny Alford. He died at age 87 in 2022. (Author's collection.)

By JIMMY MILLER

BEE BEE THE STUDENT
Bee Bee Wright, Clairton's great fistic prospect, who still is a high school student. He rushes home from his out-of-town fights to attend classes. Formerly

AND BEE BEE THE BOXER
played a halfback position on the football team, but gave it up to concentrate on boxing. He scored eight knockouts in piling up 12 consecutive victories.

Born James Maletta in Waterloo, Iowa, Bee Bee Wright (PABHOF 2020) fought out of Clairton, Pennsylvania, from 1943 to 1951. By the end of 1944, Wright was ranked by *The Ring* and possessed a 23-2 record. He beat Billy Arnold, Billy Nixon, and Al Priest but lost by final-round TKO to Kid Gavilan in 1947. Wright beat a few more contenders but retired after losing to Freddie Dawson, "Wildcat" Henry, and Terry Moore. His final record was 40-7-3, 17 KOs, and one no contest. He died in 2009 at age 83. (Author's collection.)

Tommy Yarosz (PABHOF 2015) was a 92-bout professional from Monaca, Pennsylvania, who campaigned as a middleweight and light heavyweight. During his 10-year career (1940–1950), Yarosz held a top-10 ranking in seven of those years. Although his 1948 loss to Jake LaMotta was controversial, Yarosz was never offered a rematch. One of five fighting brothers, Yarosz was featured on the cover of *The Ring* in 1949. He retired with a record of 81-10-1 (17 KOs) and died in 2006 at age 84. (Author's collection.)

25 Cents
AUGUST 1949

TOMMY YAROSZ,
One of the World's Best
Light-Heavyweights

# 5

# NON-BOXERS

Known as "The Clot" for his uncanny ability to stem bleeding cuts between rounds, Eddie Aliano (PABHOF 2009) was one of Philadelphia's greatest cutmen. Aliano worked with numerous boxers from club fighters to world champions, including Matthew Saad Muhammad and Jeff Chandler. He also trained and managed fighters early in his career. Active in the sport for 50 years, Aliano died in 1996 at age 77. (Author's collection.)

Mitch Allen (PABHOF 2014) began training boxers in 1950 after his own fighting career ended. He was a longtime coach at the Sheppard Recreation Center in West Philadelphia, where in 2005, the boxing facility was officially named the Mitchell Allen Boxing Gym. His client list included Marvin Mack, Von Clay, and great-grandson Damon Allen. His amateur fighters won 21 national championships. Allen died in 2018 at age 90. (Photograph by John DiSanto.)

James Arthur Washington was a legendary South Philadelphia trainer who went by the name Jimmy Arthur (PABHOF 2016). A gifted teacher, Arthur developed numerous boxers at the Passyunk Gym, including his son Jimmy Washington, Alfonso Hayman, Roger Russell, Frankie Mitchell, Kevin Howard, and his masterpiece, Tyrone Everett. Arthur died at age 80 in 2010. He is pictured at left with a seated Moses Robinson. (Photograph by Pete Goldfield.)

NON-BOXERS

Milt Bailey (PABHOF 2015) worked his magic as a cutman in exotic locales like Manila, Buenos Aires, and Paris as well as every major Philadelphia venue. He worked for Joe Frazier, Sonny Liston, Michael Spinks, Bennie Briscoe, and many others beginning in the early 1970s. Most famously, Bailey worked Frazier's corner against Muhammad Ali in the "Thrilla in Manila." Health issues forced his retirement in 1993. Bailey died in 2002 at age 91. (Author's collection.)

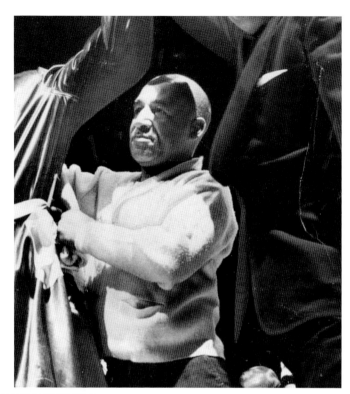

Pennsylvania native Rudy Battle (PABHOF 2020) was a busy referee who began working in Philadelphia during the 1970s. Eventually, he refereed critical bouts all over the world. Many of his best assignments occurred in Atlantic City, including world title bouts involving Bernard Hopkins, Mike Tyson, Roberto Duran, and Aaron Pryor. His biggest job was Evander Holyfield versus George Foreman in 1991. Battle, born in 1931, also judged bouts and later became Pennsylvania state boxing commissioner. (Photograph by Darryl Cobb Jr.)

Nick Belfiore (PABHOF 2006) trained and managed boxers for more than 40 years, beginning in the 1940s with his younger brother Joe Belfiore. He operated the Juniper Gym, located in South Philadelphia, where he later trained Matthew Saad Muhammad, Jeff Chandler, Mike Everett, Kevin Perry, Mike Montgomery, Bernard Peterson, and Jerry Graham. Belfiore developed Saad Muhammad from a 17-year-old street fighter into the world light heavyweight champion by age 24. Belfiore died in 1995 at age 85. (Author's collection.)

Promoter Johnny Burns (PABHOF 1962) began running boxing shows in Philadelphia around 1914. Within two years, he opened the Cambria Athletic Club and staged regular Friday night shows at the venue until his death at age 64 in 1940. "The Blood Pit" was famous for terrific fights and served as a launching pad for many future champions and contenders. Burns, who promoted hundreds of events and thousands of fights, also managed boxers, including Johnny Jadick, Joe Borrell, Nate Goldman, and Pat Haley. (Chuck Hasson.)

NON-BOXERS

Frank Cappuccino (PABHOF 1989) was a referee who saw action in Pennsylvania, Atlantic City, and around the globe. Cappuccino, born Capcino, officiated more than 500 bouts in his 50-year career (1958–2008), including championship contests involving Bernard Hopkins, Lennox Lewis, and James Toney. His biggest assignment was the 1988 heavyweight championship fight between Mike Tyson and Michael Spinks. Cappuccino was also a professional boxer (1948–1949) and a boxing judge (1958–2010). He died in 2015 at age 86. (Photograph by John DiSanto.)

Lynne Carter (PABHOF 2019) was a female trailblazer in the male-dominated sport of boxing. Carter received her license to score fights in Pennsylvania in 1982 and is still active nearly 40 years later. Some of her most high-profile scoring jobs included bouts featuring Roy Jones Jr., Bernard Hopkins, Wladimir Klitschko, Claressa Shields, Dwight Muhammad Qawi, Pernell Whitaker, Meldrick Taylor, and Lennox Lewis. Carter, born in 1952, was the second woman ever elected to the PABHOF. (Photograph by Jano Cohen.)

Born Francis Ciaccio in Brooklyn, Hank Cisco (PABHOF 1983) was a proud resident of Norristown, Pennsylvania, for most of his life. He fought professionally in the 1940s but made his name in the sport as a referee (1963–1985). Cisco was the third man in the ring for bouts featuring Joe Frazier, Matthew Saad Muhammad, Jimmy Young, Bennie Briscoe, Frank Fletcher, and Tyrone Everett. He was also a police officer and local television broadcaster. He died in 2020 at age 96. His older brother Tony Cisco (PABHOF 1984) was an 88-bout professional boxer (1935–1942). (Peltz Boxing Promotions.)

Manager Ivan Cohen (PABHOF 2019, right) began in the sport during the 1980s. He is best known for guiding Buster Drayton to the world junior middleweight championship in 1986. Cohen, born in 1947, also managed Pennsylvania light heavyweight champion Anthony Witherspoon, knockout artist Earl Hargrove, and world title challenger Tyrone Crawley. Later, he worked with Crawley's son Tyrone Crawley Jr. and his own son Brian Cohen. He is pictured with Bobby Watts (left) and Buster Drayton. (Photograph by Pete Goldfield.)

NON-BOXERS

Jack Costello's (PABHOF 1989) promising amateur boxing career was interrupted by the Korean War. After his military service, he turned to training young fighters. Costello worked out of the Harrowgate Boxing Club and the Cambria Boxing Club for 20 years before his death in 1990 at age 60. Costello also worked for the Philadelphia Electric Company for 22 years. He was a community-minded man who took his role of mentoring youth seriously. Late in life, he became a substance abuse counselor. Costello (left) is shown with boxer Hank Quinn (PABHOF 2015). (Photograph by Pete Goldfield.)

Percy "Buster" Custus (PABHOF 2017) established West Philadelphia's James Shuler Memorial Boxing Gym in 1993. He named the gym after Shuler, a rising contender and friend who tragically died in 1986 at the peak of his career. It was Shuler who encouraged Custus to get involved in the business of boxing. Custus, born in 1952, eventually trained Yusaf Mack, Dhafir Smith, Najai Turpin, Frank Walker, Rasheen Brown, and countless others who called the Shuler Gym their boxing home. (Photograph by John DiSanto.)

Announcer Ed Derian (PABHOF 2010) began working roller derby events in Philadelphia. However, his career bloomed when he started announcing local fight cards. Born Setrha Ejdaharian, Derian was a fixture at the Spectrum before following the boxing boom to Atlantic City in the late 1970s. Derian worked hundreds of casino boxing shows, many of them on national television. He continued his career until 2009, announcing in Philadelphia and Atlantic City. Derian died in 2014 at age 77. (Photograph by Pete Goldfield.)

James "Baron" Dougherty (PABHOF 2015), known as the "Baron of Leiperville," played many roles in Pennsylvania boxing. He was primarily a manager and steered Bobby Barrett and Eddie Lenny to world title fights. He also managed George Godfrey to the number-two spot in the heavyweight rankings during a time when a Black boxer could never vie for the heavyweight championship. Dougherty was also a promoter, referee, and the owner of a major training facility in Leiperville, Pennsylvania. Dougherty died in 1949 at age 80. (Richard Pagano.)

NON-BOXERS

Yancey "Yank" Durham (PABHOF 1979) was the boxing trainer who led Joe Frazier to the heavyweight championship. The tough and charismatic teacher transformed Frazier into the wrecking machine who ruled the heavyweight division for a period. His tough-love tactics in the gym also helped mold "Gypsy" Joe Harris, Willie Monroe, Mario Saurennann, Leotis Martin, and Bennie Briscoe. Durham also briefly worked with Bob Foster. He died in 1973 at age 52. (Author's collection.)

Francis X. "Pat" Duffy (PABHOF 1994) was a major force in amateur boxing. He was the manager of the 1960 and 1968 US Olympic boxing teams. He also served as the chairman of the US Amateur Athletic Union (AAU) and was a member of the Olympic committee for more than 50 years. In his various roles, he impacted the lives of countless young boxers. He died at age 94 in 2007. (Author's collection.)

THE PENNSYLVANIA BOXING HALL OF FAME

Hammond "Duke" Dugent (PABHOF 2016) was a Philadelphia police officer who ran the legendary 23rd PAL Gym beginning in 1954. The gym had a rich history as the starting point for some of Philadelphia's best fighters, including Joe Frazier, "Gypsy" Joe Harris, Bennie Briscoe, "Cyclone" Hart, Lloyd Nelson, Mario Saurennann, Al Massey, Jimmy Young, and Willie Monroe. In many cases, Dugent was their first trainer or at least played a significant role in their development. Dugent died in 1974 at age 69. He is pictured at right with Johnny Gilmore (PABHOF 2003). (Johnny Gilmore.)

After a six-bout professional career as a middleweight (1977–1984), Derek "Bozy" Ennis (PABHOF 2020) started training boxers. He established his own facility, Bozy's Dungeon, and trained Anthony Thompson, Coy Evans, Olivia Fonseca, Manny Folly, Milton Santiago Jr., Branden Pizarro, Angel Pizarro, Ray Robinson, Christian Carto, and his three sons: Derek "Pooh" Ennis, Farrah Ennis, and world champion Jaron "Boots" Ennis. Born in 1956, Ennis is still active and considered one of Philadelphia's best trainers. (Photograph by John DiSanto.)

Joey Eye (PABHOF 2015) is best known as a cutman but also held many other job titles during his more than 30 years in the sport. He was a boxer, promoter, trainer, manager, and gym proprietor. Schooled by some of Philadelphia's best cutmen, Intrieri (his real name) turned to closing cuts after his brief fighting career ended in 1993. Eye, born in 1969, is a fixture of the current fight scene, working nearly every show in the Philadelphia area. (Photograph by John DiSanto.)

As an amateur boxer, Dominic "Mickey" Grandinetti (PABHOF 2006) won three area boxing tournaments in the early 1930s. However, Grandinetti is remembered for his career as a trainer, which began around 1940. Some say the character of Mickey in the movie *Rocky* was based on him. Grandinetti, originally inducted by the spinoff Pennsylvania State Boxing Hall of Fame group, was re-inducted in 2006. He died in 1997 at age 83. He is pictured at right with heavyweight Jimmy Young. (Photograph by Pete Goldfield.)

Joe Gramby (PABHOF 2011) was a brilliant and powerful fight manager whose career spanned six decades (1930s–1990s). Philadelphia's first Black fight manager, "The Fox" flourished at a time when few opportunities existed for African Americans. He is best remembered for his association with two-time lightweight champion Bob Montgomery, but he also managed Richie Kates, "Tex" Cobb, "Honeychile" Johnson, "Chicken" Thompson, Otis Graham, Tony Thornton, Charley Scott, and Bobby Singleton. Gramby died in 1991 at age 78. He is pictured at right with Bob Montgomery. (Peltz Boxing Promotions.)

Joe Hand Sr. (PABHOF 2012) parlayed his association with Joe Frazier (as a charter shareholder in Cloverlay Incorporated) into a career in boxing promotion. Hand, a former Philadelphia police officer and detective, managed boxers and promoted live fight cards. However, his biggest impact was as a distributor of closed-circuit boxing telecasts. Hand, born in 1936, delivered live telecasts of major events to commercial establishments, including sports arenas and bars. He started his company in 1971 and still serves as the firm's chairman. (Photograph by Pete Goldfield.)

Sloan Harrison (PABHOF 2023) trained boxers for about 40 years (1980s–2020s) at various Philadelphia gyms, including the Kingsessing Recreation Center, Southwest Youth Center, Upper Darby Boxing Gym, and Marian Anderson Recreation Center. He trained Eric Hunter, Hank Lundy, Ed Dennis, Leroy Davis, Anthony Postell, and Rasheem Brown and assisted with Bernard Hopkins, Anthony Fletcher, and Damon Feldman. Harrison died in 2021 at age 71. (Photograph by John DiSanto.)

Chuck Hasson (PABHOF 2013, right) began as a boxing fan, but his passion for the sport inspired him to diligently study and record the critical details of the sweet science. Hasson, born in 1946, is considered a Philadelphia boxing authority. He produced a 12-volume compilation of newspaper clippings and magazine articles called the *Philadelphia Boxing Chronicles*. In 2002, he coauthored the book *Philadelphia's Boxing Heritage* and followed it with *Philadelphia's Boxing History Scrapbook* in 2021. Hasson is shown with Jeff Chandler (left) and "KO" Becky O'Neill. (Author's collection.)

George Hill (PABHOF 2017) started as a referee but worked more as a professional boxing judge (1989–2019). Hill scored hundreds of professional bouts, from small club shows to championship contests. Some of his assignments included fights featuring Pernell Whitaker, Wladimir Klitschko, Bernard Hopkins, Terry Norris, and Miguel Cotto. His brief fighting career (1969–1975) included sparring sessions with Joe Frazier, George Foreman, and an exhibition with Muhammad Ali. Hill died in 2021 at age 73. (Photograph by John DiSanto.)

After an amateur boxing career, George James (PABHOF 2016) was schooled by legendary manager Joe Gramby in all aspects of the sport. Although James became a trainer and assistant trainer of boxers, he preferred being called a "boxing teacher." He worked with Bennie Briscoe, "Gypsy" Joe Harris, Percy Manning, Jimmy Muse, and Richie Kates, and as exercise coach for Sonny Liston. He was devoted to boxing for more than 60 years. He died in 2017, two days before his 80th birthday. (Photograph by John DiSanto.)

NON-BOXERS

In 1976, Fred Jenkins (PABHOF 2013) followed mentor Stanley Williams as head trainer of the ABC Boxing Gym at Twenty-sixth and Master Streets in North Philadelphia. Jenkins (left), born in 1957, guided Charlie "Choo Choo" Brown (center) to the first IBF lightweight title in 1984. At 26, Jenkins was one of the youngest to train a world champion. He also worked with Rodney Moore, Marvin Garris, Jerome Jackson, Malik Scott, Zahir Raheem, Randy Griffin, Jesse Hart, and Bryant Jennings, and is still active. Marty Feldman (PABHOF 2006) is also pictured, at right. (Photograph by Pete Goldfield.)

George Katz (PABHOF 1982, left) managed many boxers in Philadelphia during his decades-long career (1930s–1960s). In the 1950s, he led welterweight Gil Turner (right) to a world title match with Kid Gavilan. Katz also managed "Kitten" Hayward, "Toothpick" Brown, Cortez Jackson, Jimmy Washington, and, for a period, Sonny Liston. Katz, a fierce defender of his fighters, was reprimanded and fined many times for ardently protesting decisions he disliked. Katz died in 1981 at age 76. (Author's collection.)

Marshall Kauffman (PABHOF 2020) began training and managing boxers out of his Kings Boxing Gym in Reading, Pennsylvania. Later, he began promoting fights. He staged shows in Philadelphia, Reading, Allentown, Harrisburg, Fort Washington, and many other locales. Kauffman, born in 1963, guided Kermit Cintron to a world title and worked with Steve Little, Julian Letterlough, Hasim Rahman, and his son Travis Kauffman. He began promoting in 1994 and is still active. (Photograph by Darryl Cobb Jr.)

Frank Kubach (PABHOF 2017, left) established the Front Street Gym with John Mulvenna and began training fighters in the early 1980s. Kubach worked with PABHOF inductees Anthony Boyle, Hank Quinn, Monty Sherrick, and Brian McGinley. Kubach, born in 1940, was elected president of the VBA–Ring One in 2019. His gym was prominently featured in the movie *Creed*. John Mulvenna (PABHOF 2013, right), born in 1950, was an amateur boxer and a Vietnam veteran before training fighters at the Hennelly Boys Club, Front Street Gym, and the Phoenixville PAL. He worked with PABHOF members Jimmy Deoria and Harry Joe Yorgey. Both Kubach and Mulvenna dedicated more than 30 years to the sport. (Photograph by Pete Goldfield.)

NON-BOXERS

Hank Kropinski (PABHOF 1994) was a ring announcer who once estimated he worked 30,000 amateur and professional bouts during his career. Born in 1928, Kropinski was immortalized in the *Guinness Book of World Records* for announcing 240 bouts in the span of one week and 96 bouts on a single day at the 1998 US Amateur Boxing Championships in Colorado Springs, Colorado. His lengthy career ended in 2006. Kropinski also served as vice president and president of the VBA–Ring One. (Photograph by Pete Goldfield.)

Stan Maliszewski (PABHOF 2018) was known to those in the boxing world as "Stan the Cutman." Part of the original Front Street Gym team, Maliszewski was taught the art of stopping cuts by Eddie Aliano. He worked with many local boxers, including Jimmy Deoria, Hank Quinn, Frankie Mitchell, Anthony Boyle, and Tony Thornton. A Vietnam veteran and professional emergency tech firefighter, Maliszewski reportedly never charged for his cutman services. He died in 2008 at age 58. (Front Street Gym.)

After a successful boxing career that included a 1961 national amateur championship and one professional bout, Woodie Marcus (PABHOF 2019) became a Philadelphia policeman. He held the job for 44 years. During that time, he became the supervisor of the PAL boxing program and served in that capacity for 39 years. Marcus, born in 1941, conducted instructional seminars, helped develop a new generation of boxing officials, and rose to the position of president of the Mid-Atlantic Boxing Association. (Author's collection.)

As Pennsylvania athletic commissioner, Howard McCall (PABHOF 1994, right) supervised boxing in the state for 12 years during two nonconsecutive stretches. McCall first took control in 1975 after Zack Clayton stepped away from the position. McCall served until 1980 when he was succeeded by James Binns (PABHOF 1994). In 1986, McCall returned as commissioner and served until his death at age 72 in 1995. He was the brother of trainer Quenzell McCall. McCall is pictured with Tim Witherspoon. (Photograph by Pete Goldfield.)

NON-BOXERS

Quenzell McCall (PABHOF 2010) won the Philadelphia Golden Gloves in 1939, placed second in the Diamond Belt tournament twice (1941 and 1942), and had a brief professional career as a boxer (1942–1943). However, his true legacy is as the trainer of Percy Bassett, Leotis Martin, Dwight Muhammad Qawi, Len Matthews, "Kitten" Hayward, Bennie Briscoe, and many others. One of the most knowledgeable boxing minds in Pennsylvania history, McCall ran the famous Champs Gym in North Philadelphia. He died in 1986 at age 65. (Photograph by Pete Goldfield.)

After his amateur boxing career, Alfred Mitchell (PABHOF 2020) became a coach around 1960. He worked with many Philadelphia boxers before becoming the head coach at the US Olympic Education Center at Northern Michigan University. Mitchell's boxers won more than 850 national amateur titles. He also trained 11 Olympians. In 1994, he was named USA Boxing Coach of the Year. Two years later, Mitchell, born in 1943, was selected as the head coach for the 1996 Olympic boxing team. (Author's collection.)

"Big" Rob Murray (PABHOF 2022) wore many hats in his 53 years in boxing. He served as a trainer, manager, advisor, matchmaker, talent scout, and mentor to many local boxers. He is credited as Bernard Hopkins's first manager and worked with Steve Little, Will Taylor, Gee Culmer, Steve Chambers, and Eddie Chambers. Murray was also a radio broadcaster and served as the director of boxing at the Blue Horizon in the 1990s and 2000s. He died in 2012 at age 67. (Photograph by John DiSanto.)

Writer Jack "KO-JO" Obermayer (PABHOF 2016) was published in *The Ring*, *Boxing Illustrated*, *Boxing Digest*, *British Boxing Weekly*, *Flash Gordon's Tonight's Boxing Program*, *Boxing Update*, and *Boxing Flash*. He also supplied records and statistics for *FightFax*. Obermayer covered 3,557 boxing shows in 402 cities during his career (1968–2016). In 2011, he received the John F.X. Condon Award for long and meritorious service from the BWAA. Obermayer died at age 72 in 2016. (Photograph by Ray Bailey.)

Frank "Blinky" Palermo (PABHOF 1982) was a notorious fight manager who maneuvered a large stable of prominent boxers, including Ike Williams, Johnny Saxton, Billy Fox, and Coley Wallace. He reached the height of his powers in the 1940s and 1950s. In 1963, Palermo was convicted of racketeering and fixing fights and was sentenced to 15 years in prison. He was paroled after eight years (1971) and lived until 1996 when he died at age 91. (Author's collection.)

Carol Polis (PABHOF 2020, right) is credited as the first-ever female boxing judge. She scored bouts in Pennsylvania, Delaware, New York, Miami, Denmark, and Venezuela. Born in 1936, Polis judged her first world title match in 1979. In her 36-year career (1973–2009), Polis scored nearly 200 bouts, 27 of them world title fights. In 2012, Polis coauthored a book about her life and career called *The Lady is a Champ*. She is pictured with Mike "Youngblood" Williams. (Carol Polis.)

Willie Reddish (PABHOF 2006, right) was a heavyweight contender (1931–1944) who faced "Jersey" Joe Walcott, Leroy Haynes, John Henry Lewis, "Tiger" Jack Fox, and Lem Franklin, and defeated Gus Dorazio, Abe Simon, Curtis Sheppard, and Elmer Ray. However, he was elected to the PABHOF as a trainer and manager for his work with Gil Turner (left), Garnet Hart, "Gypsy" Joe Harris, Curtis Parker, and Sonny Liston. Reddish died in 1988 at age 75. His son Willie Reddish Jr. (PABHOF 2018) was also a trainer. (Author's collection.)

Born Thomas A. Peed, Tommy Reed (sometimes spelled Reid, PABHOF 2022) was an outstanding referee (1969–1990) who worked in some of the most notable bouts in Philadelphia history. His assignments included Marvelous Marvin Hagler versus Bennie Briscoe, Thomas Hearns against Alfonso Hayman, Hagler versus Willie Monroe, and Bobby Chacon against Augie Pantellas. Reed started as a boxing judge in 1966 and returned to scoring fights in 1991. He retired around 1994 and died in 2005 at age 76. He is pictured with Marvelous Marvin Hagler. (Author's collection.)

NON-BOXERS

Brother Naazim Richardson (PABHOF 2014) was a respected trainer of many top-level boxers, including champions Bernard Hopkins, Steve Cunningham, Shane Mosley, and Sergio Martinez. He also was critical in the careers of many local fighters, including his sons Rock Allen and Tiger Allen and nephew Karl Dargan. Richardson famously discovered Antonio Margarito's illegal hand wraps prior to his fight with Shane Mosley in 2009. Richardson died in 2020 at age 54. (Photograph by John DiSanto.)

Adolph Ritacco (PABHOF 2019) was a cutman who worked with fighters Matthew Saad Muhammad, Joey Giardello, "Kitten" Hayward, Dan Bucceroni, Oscar Bonavena, Bud Smith, and Jimmy Carter. In 1979, his homemade blood-stemming concoctions were deemed illegal by the New Jersey State Athletic Commission. As a result, Ritacco was suspended for a period. Earlier, Ritacco was a trainer and an amateur and professional boxer. He died in 2008 at age 94. (Author's collection.)

Although "Slim" Jim Robinson (PABHOF 2015, right) could have been elected for his fighting career (two Philadelphia Diamond Belt championships and a solid professional record), he made a larger impact as a trainer. Robinson guided Tim Witherspoon and Mike Rossman to world titles and worked with Eddie Mustafa Muhammad, Rickey Parkey, Alfonso Ratliff, Curtis Parker, and Azumah Nelson. He died at age 74 in 2004. Robinson is shown with Mike Rossman. (Author's collection.)

Along Boxing Front—

# 'Slug Alley' Promoters Say 'Best Fight Town' Hits Pocket Book Hard

### By CARL HUGHES

Pittsburgh is the best fight town in the country, ye it's one of the few spots where the beak-breaking busines is not booming. Why? That's what Art Rooney anc Barney McGinley would like to know.

Art Rooney and Barney McGinley (both PABHOF 2019) were partners in one of the most successful promotional companies in boxing history. Beginning in the late 1930s, they ruled Pittsburgh boxing for almost 20 years. In the 1950s, they staged shows headlined by Billy Conn, Charley Burley, Sammy Angott, Fritzie Zivic, Teddy Yarosz, and Jackie Wilson. They promoted or co-promoted huge events at Forbes Field, including "Jersey" Joe Walcott's title-winning knockout of Ezzard Charles in 1951. They also co-owned the National Football League's Pittsburgh Steelers. Rooney died in 1988 at age 87, and McGinley died in 1953 at age 64. (Author's collection.)

NON-BOXERS

William "Pinny" Schafer (PABHOF 2006) was a fight manager best known for his association with heavyweight contender Leotis Martin during the 1960s. He guided Martin to a heavyweight championship tournament and an upset of Sonny Liston. Schafer also worked with boxers Sammy Goss, Marty Feldman, and Bennie Briscoe. His career outside of boxing was as a bartender and union organizer. Schafer was the president of the Bartenders Local Union for 14 years. He died in 1976 at age 61. Schafer (left) is shown with Bennie Briscoe. (Johnny Gilmore.)

Born in 1933, Augie Scimeca (PABHOF 2016) is best known as a gym proprietor and the manager and co-trainer of world champion Charles Brewer. He also worked with Tyrone Crawley, Calvin Grove, Earl Hargrove, Buster Drayton, and Ramon Santana. The South Philadelphia native started in 1954 as an assistant trainer at the Mickey Rosati Gym. He moved over to the Passyunk Gym for 15 years before opening his own place. "Augie's Gym" was a busy facility until Scimeca's retirement in 2005. (Author's collection.)

Born Joseph Schabacker in Germany, Joe Shannon (PABHOF 1979) came to the United States in 1903 as a child. Shannon began fighting as an amateur around 1916 and turned professional around 1923. After his fighting career ended, he served as a boxing judge and referee. In 1935, he was a founding member of the VBA–Ring One and was elected president of the organization in 1939. Shannon died at age 94 in 1995. (Author's collection.)

Sam Solomon (PABHOF 2015, left) was a Philadelphia Golden Gloves champion with a reported 300 amateur bouts. Instead of boxing professionally, Solomon played professional baseball for the Negro League's Central Stars. He became a boxing trainer around 1950 and worked with outstanding fighters, including "Cyclone" Hart, Matthew Saad Muhammad, Jesse Smith, Ernie Terrell (right), Leon Spinks, Trevor Berbick, and Leslie Stewart during his career. Solomon died in 1998 at age 83. (Author's collection.)

Joe Sweeney (PABHOF 1979), pictured counting out Tom Brown, had a career as a professional welterweight before making his mark as a referee and judge. He refereed at least 250 bouts in Pennsylvania (1937–1972), including Joey Giardello versus Henry Hank II, Charley Scott versus Garnet Hart, and "Kitten" Hayward against Bennie Briscoe I. His biggest event was the heavyweight championship fight between Joe Frazier and Oscar Bonavena at the Spectrum in 1968. He died in 1986 at age 73. (Author's collection.)

Leon Tabbs (PABHOF 2014) was an amateur boxer before he began training fighters while serving in the US Army. After his military service, he trained professional Jerry Martin and others. However, his largest contribution was as a cutman. Tabbs is best known for his work with Bernard Hopkins, whom he worked for exclusively in his later years. He also became a pioneer cutman in mixed martial arts. Tabbs retired from both sports in 2013 and died in 2018 at age 86. (Photograph by John DiSanto.)

Anthony "Pete" Tomasco (PABHOF 1976) was a referee who worked many key bouts during his long career. In 1952, he refereed the welterweight championship fight between Kid Gavilan and Gil Turner. He also was the referee for fights involving Joey Giardello, George Benton (left), Harold Johnson, Tyrone Everett, and Mike Rossman. His days as a referee ended in the mid-1970s. Tomasco died in 1984 at age 75. (Peltz Boxing Promotions.)

Jimmy Toppi Sr. (PABHOF 1975) was a boxing promoter and manager for 40 years. He began staging fights in 1926, running shows in many Philadelphia venues, especially long stints at the New Broadway Arena and the Olympia Athletic Club. In his time, Toppi promoted legends Benny Bass, Midget Wolgast, Bob Montgomery, Gus Dorazio, "Gypsy" Joe Harris, Willie Pep, Joe Frazier, Luis Rodriguez, and Bennie Briscoe. Toppi died in 1967 at age 68 while still an active promoter. Pictured is Toppi's Philadelphia office building. (Peltz Boxing Promotions.)

NON-BOXERS

Trainer Carey "Pop Bates" Williams (PABHOF 2018) reportedly lost a leg in an accident during his days as a bootlegger. The prosthesis he wore hampered his ability to get in and out of the ring quickly. Therefore, despite his vast knowledge, Williams was relegated to handling the bucket and stool during fights. He was head trainer at the Passyunk Gym for many years and was a mentor to trainer Jimmy Arthur. Williams died in 1985 at age 73. (Photograph by Pete Goldfield.)

Born Vincent Silvano, Jimmy Wilson (PABHOF 2009) was an accomplished cutman and trainer who worked with many excellent boxers, including champions Ike Williams, Lew Jenkins, Sonny Liston, and Johnny Saxton, and contenders Gus Dorazio and Billy Fox. Wilson died suddenly in 1958 at age 54 while still in his prime as a cornerman. He also had a modest professional career as a welterweight boxer (1919–1926). (George Silvano.)

# PENNSYLVANIA BOXING
# HALL OF FAME INDUCTEES
## 1958–2023

Billy Abel Sr.
Mike Acri
Sidney Adams
John Aiello
Eddie Aliano
Mitch Allen
Benny Amparo
Sammy Angott
Billy Arnold
Jimmy Arthur
Jerome Artis
Joe Aurillo
Milt Bailey
Bob Baker
Teddy Baldwin
Bobby Barrett
Carmen Bartolomeo
Benny Bass
Percy Bassett
Rudy Battle
Joey Belfiore
Leland Beloff
Richie Bennett
George Benton
Tony Bersani
David Bey
Tyrell Biggs
Jimmy Binns
Johnny Bizzarro
Lou Bizzarro
Jack Blackburn
Lucien Blackwell
Harry Blitman
Harry Bobo
Joe Bonadies
George Bonner

Bill Bossio
Anthony Boyle
Pat Bradley
Patsy Bradley
Johnny Brenda
Charles Brewer
Bennie Briscoe
Jackie Britton
Charlie Brown
Harry Brown
Henry Brown
Santa Bucca
Dan Bucceroni
Vinny Burgese
Charley Burley
Jimmy Burns
Johnny Burns
Whit Burress
Dom Burrone
Ernie Caesar
Frank Cappuccino
Vic Capcino
Frankie Caris
Jimmy Carlini
John Carroll
John "Lefty" Carroll
Johnny Carter
Lynne Carter
Frankie Carto
Nunzio Carto
Rocky Castellani
James Cavanaugh
Harry Cavella
Joe Cervino
Jeff Chandler
George Chavanne Sr.

George Chip
Hank Cisco
Tony Cisco
Ralph Citro
Johnny Clark
Randall Cobb
Frankie Cocco
Ivan Cohen
Nigel Collins
Billy Conn
Eddie Cool
Bert Cooper
Matthew Copplino
Eddie Corma
Jack Costello
Tyrone Crawley
Joe Crosly
Tommy Cross
Buck Crouse
Angel Cruz
Charlie Cummings
Willie Curry
Tom Cushman
Buster Custus
Fred D'Angelo
Wee Willie Davies
Billy Davis
Bobby Dean
Bucky DeCarlo
Cuddy DeMarco
Sal DeMeo
Jimmy Deoria
Jim Deoria Sr.
Ed Derian
Vic Diamond
Rudy Donato

Gus Dorazio
Danny Dougherty
James Dougherty
Buster Drayton
Yank Durham
Pat Duffy
Duke Dugent
Angelo Dundee
Bat Dundee
Chris Dundee
Don Elbaum
Al Ettore
Bozy Ennis
Derek Ennis
Young Erne
Charlie Ettinger
Mike Evans
Mike Everett
Tyrone Everett
Joey Eye
Joe Fagan
Tony Falco
Chick Feldman
Marty Feldman
Al Fennell
Bernard Fernandez
Gerry Finnerty
Bouie Fisher
Anthony Fletcher
Frank Fletcher
Troy Fletcher
Johnny Forte
Tommy Forte
Nat Frank
Joe Frazier
Marvis Frazier
Jacqui Frazier-Lyde
Marvin Garris
Battling Gates
Joey Giardello
Willie Gibbs
Johnny Gilmore
Eddie Giosa
George Godfrey

Gene Gollotto
Mickey Grandinetti
Randy Griffin
Sammy Goss
Otis Graham
Joe Gramby
Robert Grasso
Harry Greb
Tony Green
Calvin Grove
Joe Guinan
Joe Hand Sr.
Earl Hargrove
J.J. Harrington
"Gypsy" Joe Harris
Sloan Harrison
Eugene Hart
Garnet Hart
Chuck Hasson
Jack Hauf
Frankie Hayes
Johnny Hayes
Alfonso Hayman
Stanley Hayward
Gary Hegyi
Sam Hickman
George Hill
Robert Hines
Wade Hinnant
Gary Hinton
Stan Hochman
Larry Holmes
Mark Holmes
Vaughn Hooks
Bernard Hopkins
Art Hosefros
Leo Houck
Kevin Howard
Johnny Hughes
Robert Hurst
Johnny Hutchinson
John David Jackson
Johnny Jadick
Lou Jaffe

George James
Fred Jenkins
Harold Johnson
William Jones
Jerry Judge
Kerry Judge
Richie Kates
George Katz
Benny Kauffman
Marshall Kauffman
Hugh Kearney
Ed Keenan
Freddie Kelly
Kelvin Kelly
Pete Kelly
Teon Kennedy
Frank Klaus
Danny Kramer
Frank Kubach
Hank Kropinski
Ralph Lake
George Larover
Pete Latzo
Dorsey Lay
Franny Lederer
Bernard Lemisch
Jackie Lennon
Julian Letterlough
Battling Levinsky
Harry Lewis
Sonny Liston
Steve Little
Pete Logue
Young Loughery
Frank Loughrey
Tommy Loughran
Tommy Lowry
Marvin Mack
Yusaf Mack
Billy Maher
Peter Maher
Tommy Maher
Stan Maliszewski
Percy Manning

Tommy Marciano
Woodie Marcus
Mickey Martell
Richie Martell
Jerry Martin
Leotis Martin
Tony Martin
Freddy Martucci
Al Massey
Lew Massey
Len Matthews
Fritz McBride
Howard McCall
Quenzell McCall
Jack McCarron
Joey McCausland
Jack McClelland
John McCullough
Lanse McCurley
Jack McKinney
Brian McGinley
Barney McGinley
Terry McGovern
Jack McGuigan
Joe McIntyre
Johnny Mealey
Marty Mellett
Jimmy Mendo
Nate Miller
Alfred Mitchell
Dick Mitchell
Willie Monroe
Bob Montgomery
Harold Moore
Pal Moore
Reddy Moore
Rodney Moore
Willie Moore
Michael Moorer
Frank Moran
Bobby Morgano
Tony Morgano
Johnny Morris
Wesley Mouzon

John Mulvenna
Battling Murray
Rob Murray
Luigi Napolitano
Johnny Natchez
Ed Nodler
Jimmy Oakland
Jack Obermayer
Philadelphia Jack O'Brien
Jack O'Halloran
Joe O'Neill
Tommy O'Toole
Mayon Padlo
Frank Palermo
Alex Palumbo
Frank Palumbo
Augie Pantellas
Curtis Parker
Willie Patterson
John Paxton
Gennaro Pellegrini
J Russell Peltz
Arthur R. Pelullo
Freddie Pendleton
Johnny Pepe
Ed Petrone
Ernie Petrone
Mike Picciotti
Joe Polino
Carol Polis
Andre Prophet
Kid Primo
Dwight Muhammad Qawi
Hank Quinn
Franny Rafferty
Zahir Raheem
Willie Reddish
Willie Reddish Jr.
Tommy Reed
David Reid
Freddie Reyes
Naazim Richardson
Adolph Ritacco
Young Robideau

Ivan Robinson
Slim Jim Robinson
Billy Rocap
Ed Rodger
Fernando Rodriguez
Art Rooney
Mickey Rosati
Mike Rossman
Joe Rowan
Roger Russell
Babe Ruth
Tommy Ruth
Matthew Saad Muhammad
Phil Sacks
Lee Sala
Freddie Sammons
Joe Sankey
Charles Santore
Mario Saurennann
Pinny Schafer
Augie Scimeca
Charley Scott
Monty Sherrick
James Shuler
Charles Sgrillo
Joe Shannon
Curtis Sheppard
Ernie Singletary
Charles Singleton
Lew Skymer
Billy Smith
Gunboat Smith
Jesse Smith
Sammy Smith
Steve Smoger
Frank Snockey
Frankie Sodano
Sam Solomon
Young King Solomon
Jimmy Soo
Billy Soose
Paul Spadafora
Nick Spano
Billy Speary

Michael Spinks
Joe Stafford
Joey Stano
Tony Stenza
Jimmy Stewart
John Stewart
Mike Stewart
Tony Strazzeri
Maxie Strub
Barry Stumpf
Tony Suerro
Joe Sweeney
Jimmie Sykes
Leon Tabbs
Herman Taylor
Meldrick Taylor
Myron Taylor
Will Taylor
Lew Tendler
Angelo Testa
Joe Thomas
Elvin Thompson
Tony Thornton
Dave Tiberi
Pete Tomasco
Jimmy Toppi
Larry Torpey
Norman Torpey Sr.
Steve Traitz Jr.
Steve Traitz Sr.
Al Trainor
Joe Trainor
Joe Trofe
Chucky Tschorniawsky
Dick Turner
Gil Turner
Jimmy Tygh
Chicky Veasey
Henry Von Savage
Jersey Joe Walcott
Billy Wallace
Bobby Watts
Frank Weiner
Dick Welsh

Ike White
Carey Williams
Roy Williams
Jackie Wilson
Jimmy Wilson
Joe Wilton
Frank Windy
Anthony Witherspoon
Tim Witherspoon
Henry Wolfe
Bobby Wolgast
Johnny Wolgast
Midget Wolgast
Eddie Woods
Bee Bee Wright
Tom Yankello
Jimmy Young
Teddy Yarosz
Tommy Yarosz
Harry Joe Yorgey
Dave Zinkoff
Fritzie Zivic

# Discover Thousands of Local History Books
## Featuring Millions of Vintage Images

Arcadia Publishing, the leading local history publisher in the United States, is committed to making history accessible and meaningful through publishing books that celebrate and preserve the heritage of America's people and places.

Find more books like this at
**www.arcadiapublishing.com**

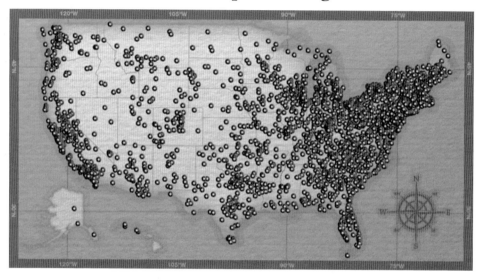

Search for your hometown history, your old stomping grounds, and even your favorite sports team.

Consistent with our mission to preserve history on a local level, this book was printed in South Carolina on American-made paper and manufactured entirely in the United States. Products carrying the accredited Forest Stewardship Council (FSC) label are printed on 100 percent FSC-certified paper.

**MADE IN THE**